INTRODUCTION

This short book explains how a felony prison sentence is served in North Carolina. I hope those who read it will gain a better sense of where and how an inmate serves his or her time.

Presenting the information in illustrated form is by no means intended to make light of a very serious subject. It is, rather, offered as an accessible way to fill gaps in knowledge and to address common misperceptions about the way sentences are served. It is meant to give crime victims, defendants, inmates, and their families an understandable resource that translates the words and numbers on a sentencing judgment into a practical reality.

Though the book is of course not a comprehensive legal reference, I hope it will be useful to lawyers and judges, too. An improved understanding of how a sentence is administered should help you advise your clients, negotiate your pleas, and craft your judgments in a way that achieves a more refined measure of justice in each case.

I have neither the technical expertise nor the artistic talent to create something like this on my own. For the former, I relied on co-author Shane Tharrington, classification manager for North Carolina's Division of Adult Correction. For the latter, I turned to Jason Whitley, a talented illustrator who works as a creative lead for instructional innovation at the Eshelman School of Pharmacy at UNC-Chapel Hill. Many thanks to Shane (and to the prison system as a whole) for answering my many questions, and to Jason for turning my stick-figure storyboard into a real graphic novel.

Jamie Markham
Chapel Hill
September 2017

ISSUE NO. 1

JULY 2017

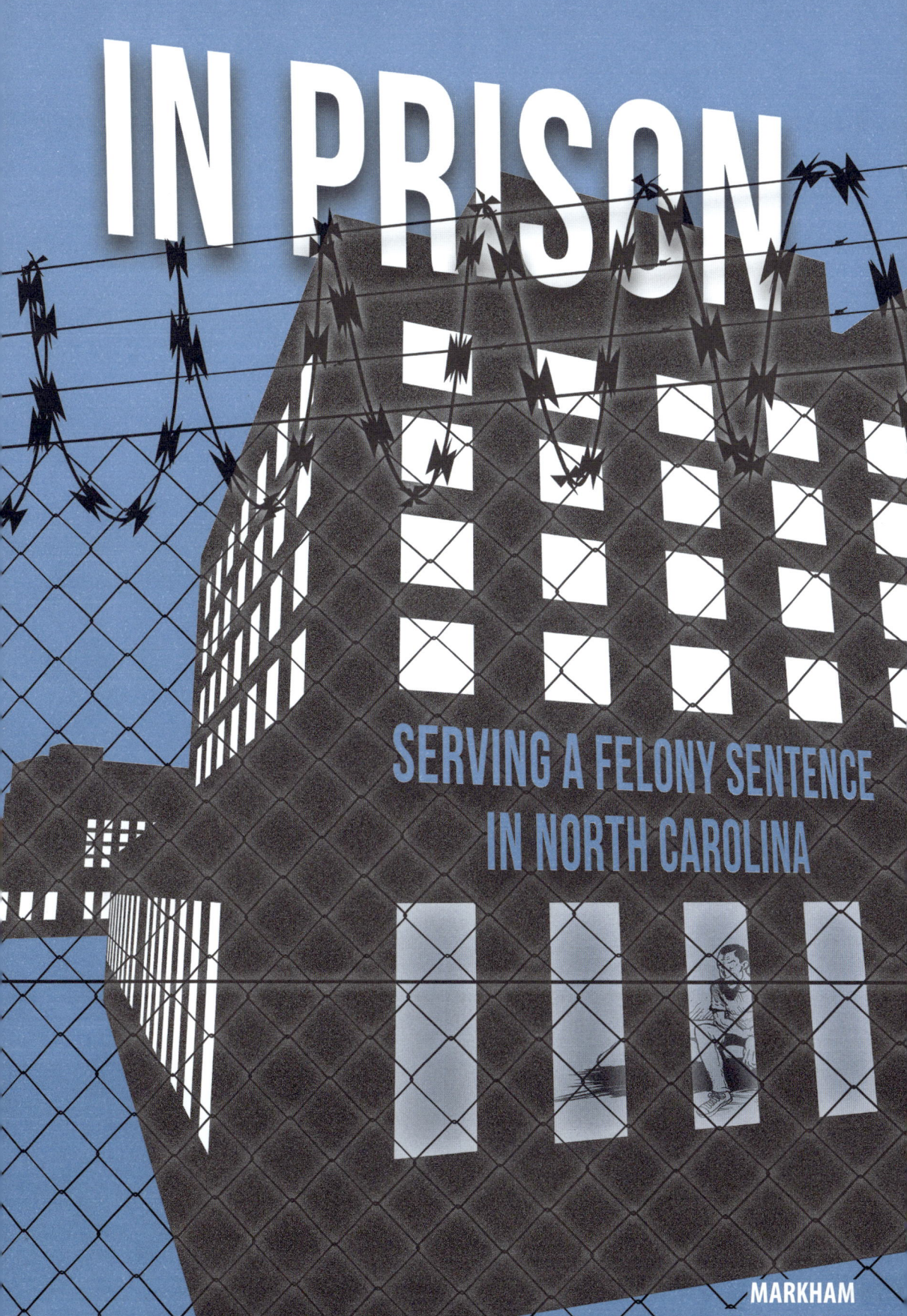

IN PRISON

SERVING A FELONY SENTENCE IN NORTH CAROLINA

MARKHAM
THARRINGTON
WHITLEY

The School of Government at the University of North Carolina at Chapel Hill works to improve the lives of North Carolinians by engaging in practical scholarship that helps public officials and citizens understand and improve state and local government. Established in 1931 as the Institute of Government, the School provides educational, advisory, and research services for state and local governments. The School of Government is also home to a nationally ranked Master of Public Administration program, the North Carolina Judicial College, and specialized centers focused on community and economic development, information technology, and environmental finance.

As the largest university-based local government training, advisory, and research organization in the United States, the School of Government offers up to 200 courses, webinars, and specialized conferences for more than 12,000 public officials each year. In addition, faculty members annually publish approximately 50 books, manuals, reports, articles, bulletins, and other print and online content related to state and local government. The School also produces the *Daily Bulletin Online* each day the General Assembly is in session, reporting on activities for members of the legislature and others who need to follow the course of legislation.

Operating support for the School of Government's programs and activities comes from many sources, including state appropriations, local government membership dues, private contributions, publication sales, course fees, and service contracts.

Visit sog.unc.edu or call 919.966.5381 for more information on the School's courses, publications, programs, and services.

© 2017
School of Government
The University of North Carolina at Chapel Hill

Printed in the United States of America

21 20 19 18 17   1 2 3 4 5

ISBN 978-1-56011-899-2

∞ This publication is printed on permanent, acid-free paper in compliance with the North Carolina General Statutes.

♲ Printed on recycled paper

THE DEFENDANT WILL BE HELD IN THE COUNTY JAIL UNTIL THE PRISON SYSTEM PICKS HIM UP, USUALLY WITHIN A WEEK OR SO.

IF THE DEFENDANT APPEALS HIS SENTENCE, HE COULD BE RELEASED ON AN APPEAL BOND, BUT THAT IS RARE.

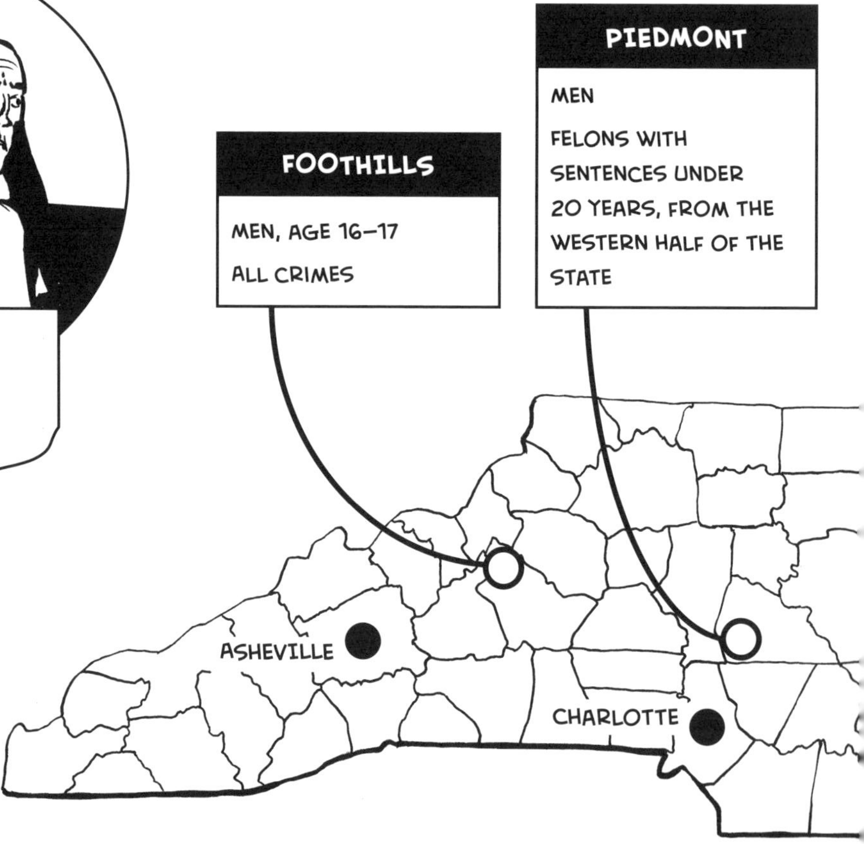

THE DEFENDANT'S FIRST STOP WILL BE ONE OF NORTH CAROLINA'S DIAGNOSTIC CENTERS.

FOOTHILLS

MEN, AGE 16–17
ALL CRIMES

PIEDMONT

MEN

FELONS WITH SENTENCES UNDER 20 YEARS, FROM THE WESTERN HALF OF THE STATE

ASHEVILLE

CHARLOTTE

NORTH CAROLINA'S DIAGNOSTIC CENTERS

THE DEFENDANT GENERALLY WILL GET JAIL CREDIT FOR ALL THE DAYS HE SPENT IN JAIL BEFORE CONVICTION.

JAIL CREDIT IS SUBTRACTED FROM BOTH THE MINIMUM AND MAXIMUM SENTENCE. FOR EXAMPLE, IF THE DEFENDANT HAD 2 MONTHS OF JAIL CREDIT, HE WOULD HAVE 8–19 MONTHS LEFT TO SERVE OF HIS 10–21 MONTH SENTENCE.

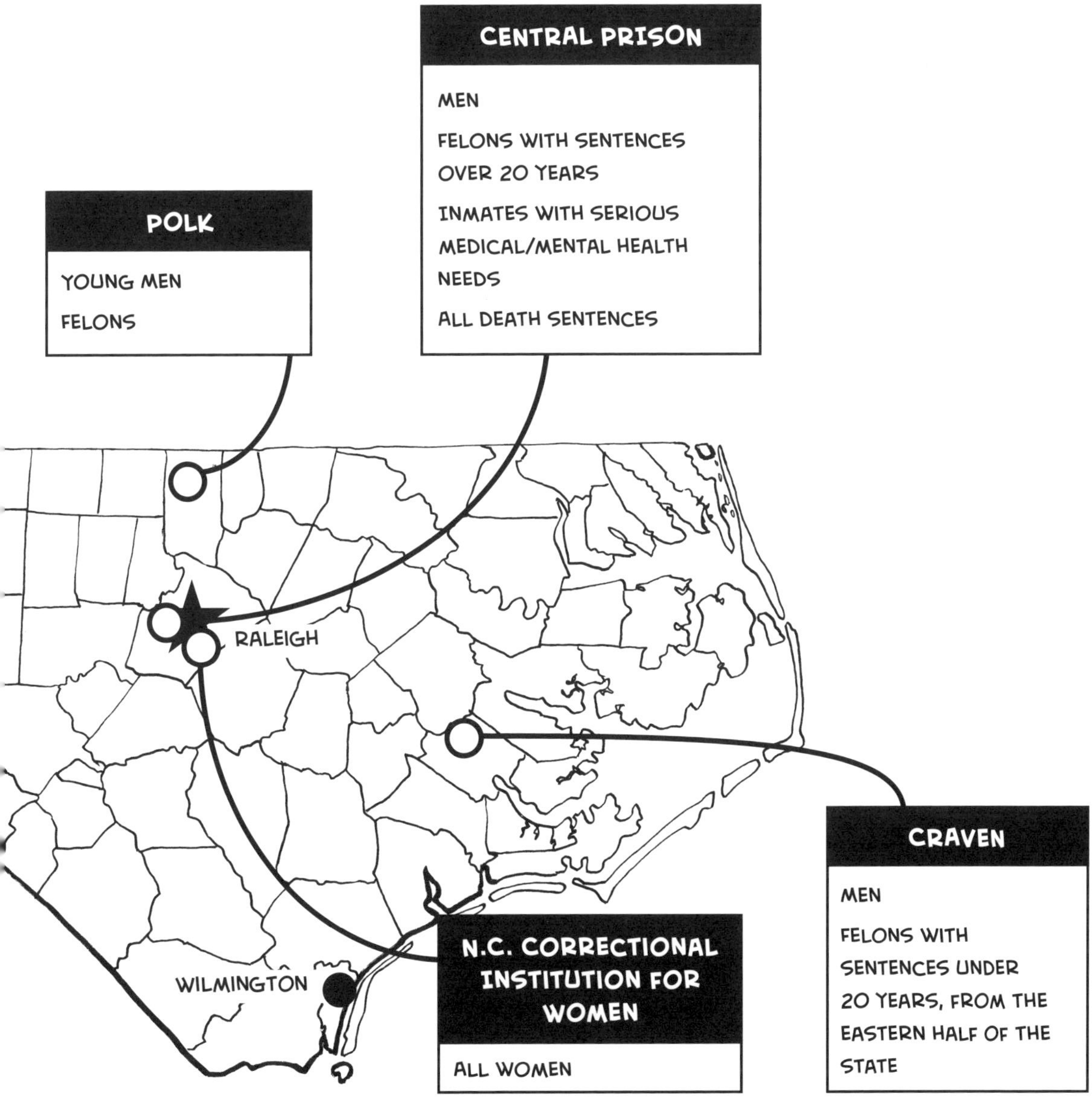

CENTRAL PRISON

MEN

FELONS WITH SENTENCES OVER 20 YEARS

INMATES WITH SERIOUS MEDICAL/MENTAL HEALTH NEEDS

ALL DEATH SENTENCES

POLK

YOUNG MEN

FELONS

RALEIGH

WILMINGTON

CRAVEN

MEN

FELONS WITH SENTENCES UNDER 20 YEARS, FROM THE EASTERN HALF OF THE STATE

N.C. CORRECTIONAL INSTITUTION FOR WOMEN

ALL WOMEN

THE DEFENDANT WILL SPEND 2-4 WEEKS AT THE DIAGNOSTIC FACILITY COMPLETING VARIOUS INPROCESSING ACTIVITES.

CLOTHING EXCHANGE

FINGERPRINTING

RISK-NEEDS ASSESSMENT

DNA SAMPLE

EYE EXAM

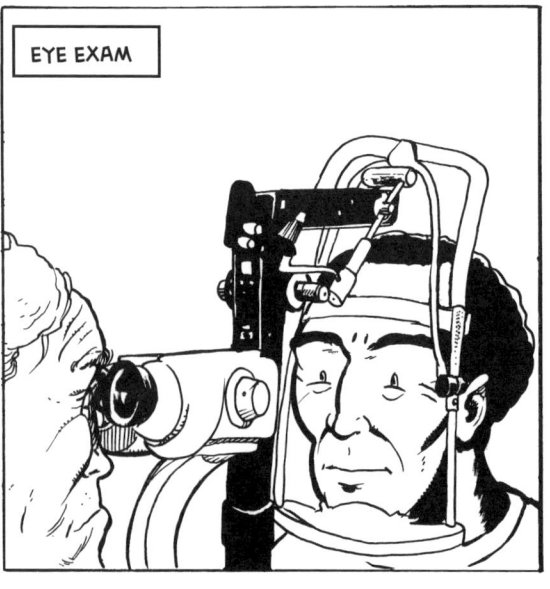

INTELLIGENCE TESTING

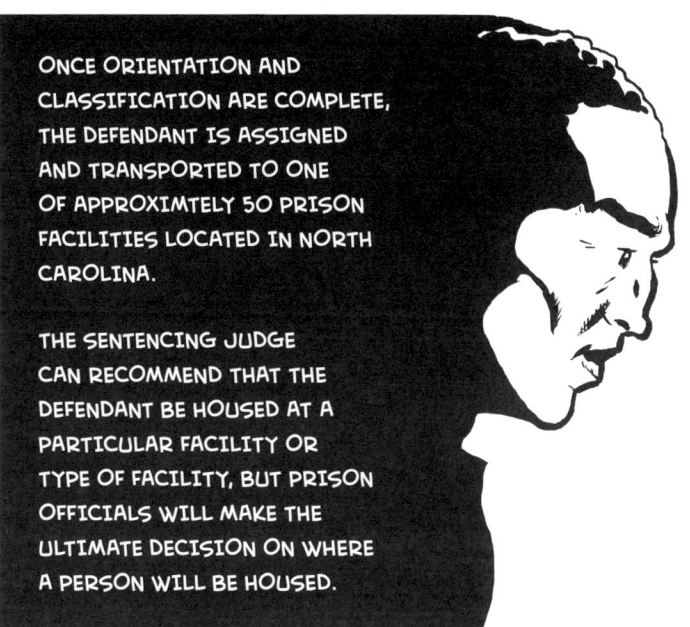

ONCE ORIENTATION AND CLASSIFICATION ARE COMPLETE, THE DEFENDANT IS ASSIGNED AND TRANSPORTED TO ONE OF APPROXIMTELY 50 PRISON FACILITIES LOCATED IN NORTH CAROLINA.

THE SENTENCING JUDGE CAN RECOMMEND THAT THE DEFENDANT BE HOUSED AT A PARTICULAR FACILITY OR TYPE OF FACILITY, BUT PRISON OFFICIALS WILL MAKE THE ULTIMATE DECISION ON WHERE A PERSON WILL BE HOUSED.

THE HOUSING DECISION IS BASED IN PART ON THE CUSTODY LEVEL TO WHICH THE INMATE IS ASSIGNED DURING CLASSIFICATION.

THERE ARE THREE MAIN CUSTODY LEVELS IN THE NORTH CAROLINA PRISON SYSTEM:

CLOSE CUSTODY (MOST SECURE)

MEDIUM CUSTODY

MINIMUM CUSTODY

THE MAP BELOW SHOWS SOME OF THE PRISONS TO WHICH AN INMATE MIGHT BE ASSIGNED. IT HIGHLIGHTS A SAMPLING OF THE SPECIAL PROGRAMS AND JOB ASSIGNMENTS AVAILABLE AT CERTAIN PRISONS. OVER THE COURSE OF SERVING A SENTENCE, SOME INMATES WILL TRANSFER BETWEEN FACILITIES AS CUSTODY LEVELS, WORK ASSIGNMENTS, AND PROGRAM NEEDS CHANGE.

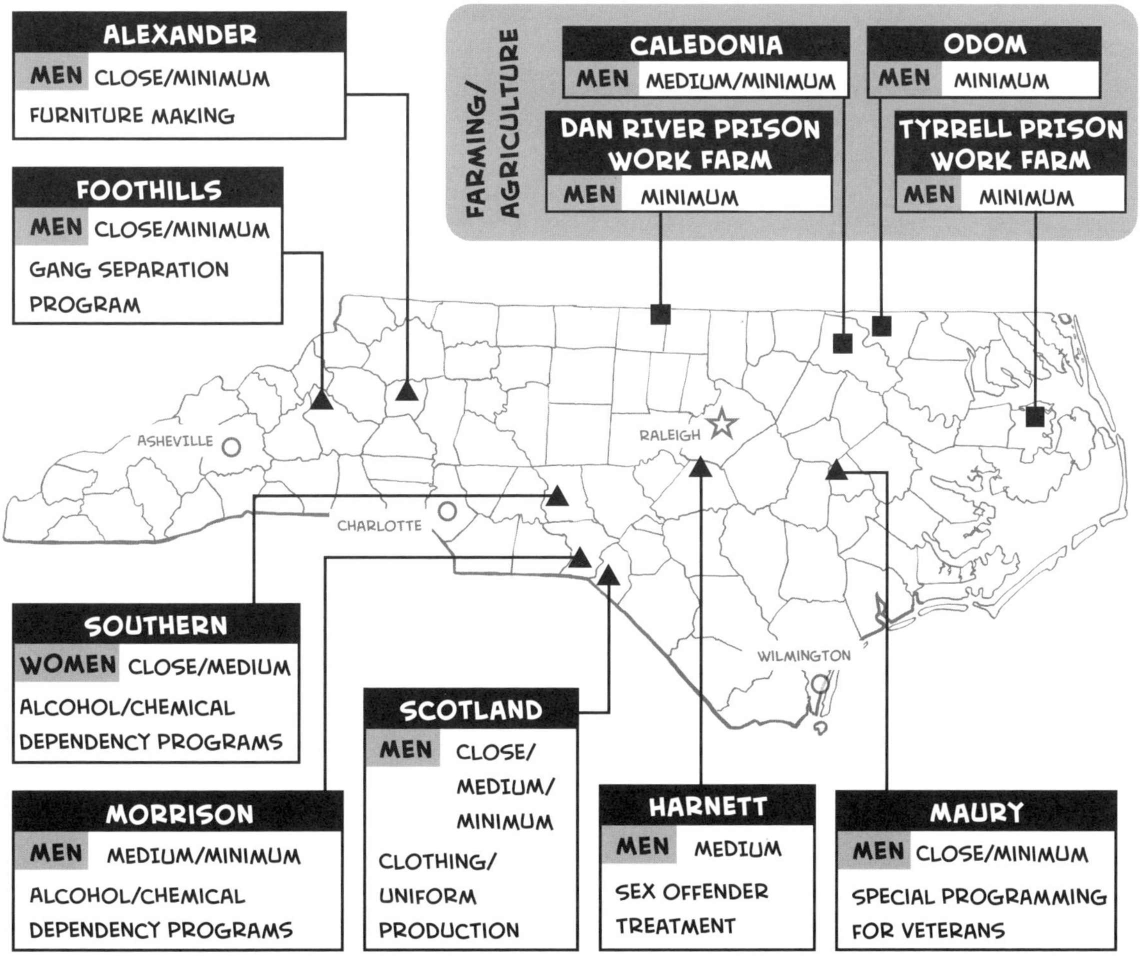

ALEXANDER
MEN CLOSE/MINIMUM
FURNITURE MAKING

FOOTHILLS
MEN CLOSE/MINIMUM
GANG SEPARATION PROGRAM

FARMING/AGRICULTURE

CALEDONIA
MEN MEDIUM/MINIMUM

DAN RIVER PRISON WORK FARM
MEN MINIMUM

ODOM
MEN MINIMUM

TYRRELL PRISON WORK FARM
MEN MINIMUM

ASHEVILLE

RALEIGH

CHARLOTTE

WILMINGTON

SOUTHERN
WOMEN CLOSE/MEDIUM
ALCOHOL/CHEMICAL DEPENDENCY PROGRAMS

MORRISON
MEN MEDIUM/MINIMUM
ALCOHOL/CHEMICAL DEPENDENCY PROGRAMS

SCOTLAND
MEN CLOSE/ MEDIUM/ MINIMUM
CLOTHING/ UNIFORM PRODUCTION

HARNETT
MEN MEDIUM
SEX OFFENDER TREATMENT

MAURY
MEN CLOSE/MINIMUM
SPECIAL PROGRAMMING FOR VETERANS

AT THE ASSIGNED FACILITY, THE INMATE BEGINS SERVING THE REMAINDER OF HIS SENTENCE. HOW LONG IT WILL TAKE TO SERVE IT DEPENDS IN PART ON WHAT HE DOES IN PRISON. PARTICIPATION IN WORK AND PROGRAMS ALLOWS AN INMATE TO EARN SENTENCE CREDITS CALLED **EARNED TIME**.

EARNED TIME IS AWARDED AT DIFFERENT RATES DEPENDING ON THE TYPE OF WORK OR PROGRAM COMPLETED. IN GENERAL, PARTICIPATION IN ANY OF THE JOBS OR PROGRAMS SHOWN BELOW WOULD BE REWARDED WITH 9 DAYS OF EARNED TIME PER MONTH.

EDUCATIONAL PROGRAMS

LAUNDRY

LICENSE PLATES

CONSTRUCTION

CUSTODIAL WORK

AN INMATE AWAITING A WORK OR PROGRAM ASSIGNMENT GENERALLY GETS 3 DAYS OF EARNED TIME PER MONTH.

INMATES CAN ALSO GET ANOTHER CREDIT CALLED **MERITORIOUS TIME** FOR EXEMPLARY ACTS, LIKE WORKING IN BAD WEATHER OR COMPLETING AN EDUCATIONAL DEGREE.

WELDING

ROAD SIGNS

TREATMENT GROUP

DOG TRAINING

ROAD WORK

KITCHEN WORK

SO WHEN IS AN INMATE RELEASED?

FELONY ACTIVE SENTENCES HAVE TWO PARTS: A PERIOD OF CONFINEMENT IN PRISON, FOLLOWED BY A PERIOD OF **POST-RELEASE SUPERVISION** (PRS). PRS IS A PERIOD OF SUPERVISED RELEASE IN THE COMMUNITY, SIMILAR TO PROBATION.

THE LENGTH OF THE PRS PORTION OF THE SENTENCE DEPENDS ON THE INMATE'S CLASS OF OFFENSE AND WHETHER OR NOT THE CRIME REQUIRES REGISTRATION AS A SEX OFFENDER.

OFFENSE CLASS	PRS PORTION OF MAXIMUM
CLASS F–I	9 MONTHS
CLASS B1–E	12 MONTHS
CLASS B1–E SEX CRIME	60 MONTHS

THE PRISON SYSTEM AUTOMATICALLY SUBTRACTS THE PRS PORTION OF THE SENTENCE FROM THE MAXIMUM AND SETS IT OFF TO THE SIDE. THAT'S BECAUSE THE INMATE WILL SERVE THAT TIME ONLY IF HIS POST-RELEASE SUPERVISION IS REVOKED. THE TIME THAT REMAINS AFTER SUBTRACTING THE PRS PORTION IS THE CONFINEMENT PORTION OF THE SENTENCE—THE TIME THE PERSON WILL ACTUALLY SPEND IN PRISON.

⬇ MAXIMUM SENTENCE ⬇

SOME PEOPLE THINK ALL INMATES ARE RELEASED ONCE THEY HAVE SERVED THEIR MINIMUM SENTENCE. **THEY AREN'T**. INSTEAD, THE INMATE STARTS FROM THE MAXIMUM AND WORKS HIS WAY DOWN THROUGH EARNED TIME AND MERITORIOUS TIME.

EXIT

MINIMUM SENTENCE

THE MINIMUM SENTENCE IS JUST THE LOWER LIMIT ON HOW MUCH THE SENTENCE MAY BE REDUCED. IN OTHER WORDS, NO MATTER HOW MUCH WORK HE DOES OR HOW MANY PROGRAMS HE COMPLETES, THE INMATE WILL NOT BE RELEASED BEFORE SERVING HIS MINIMUM SENTENCE.

MOST INMATES ARE NOT ABLE TO WORK THEIR SENTENCES ALL THE WAY DOWN TO THE MINIMUM. AVERAGE RELEASE DATES FOR EACH CLASS OF FELONY ARE SHOWN IN THE TABLE BELOW.

OFFENSE CLASS	PERCENT OF MINIMUM SERVED UPON RELEASE...
CLASS B1–C	102%
CLASS D	103%
CLASS E	104%
CLASS F	105%
CLASS G	107%
CLASS H	114%
CLASS I	113%

NOTICE THAT INMATES WITH MORE SERIOUS CONVICTIONS GENERALLY DO A BETTER JOB OF WORKING THEIR RELEASE DATES DOWN TOWARD THE MINIMUM SENTENCE. WHY? IT'S BECAUSE MANY INMATES WITH SHORTER SENTENCES AREN'T IN PRISON LONG ENOUGH TO COMPLETE PROGRAMS OR GET PLACED IN THE JOBS THAT EARN A LOT OF EARNED TIME.

LET'S PUT IT ALL TOGETHER FOR OUR EXAMPLE OF AN INMATE SERVING A 10–21 MONTH SENTENCE FOR A CLASS G FELONY. THE LAST 9 MONTHS OF HIS SENTENCE WILL BE SET ASIDE FOR PRS, LEAVING 10–12 MONTHS OF CONFINEMENT TO SERVE. ON AVERAGE, AN INMATE WITH A SENTENCE LIKE THAT WILL SERVE 107% OF HIS MINIMUM (10.7 MONTHS IN THIS CASE) BEFORE BEING RELEASED ONTO PRS. THE EARLIEST POSSIBLE RELEASE IS 10 MONTHS. THE LATEST IS 12 MONTHS.

10–12 MONTHS

CONFINEMENT PORTION

9 MONTHS

PRS PORTION

A FELONY INMATE'S SENTENCE IS NOT COMPLETE UPON RELEASE. ALL FELONS SERVE A TERM OF POST-RELEASE SUPERVISION (PRS) AFTER THEY ARE RELEASED FROM PRISON. IT'S MANDATORY—THE INMATE CANNOT REFUSE IT. THE LENGTH OF THE PRS TERM IS GOVERNED BY THE TYPE OF SENTENCE.

OFFENSE CLASS	LENGTH OF PRS
CLASS F–I	9 MONTHS
CLASS B1–E	12 MONTHS
SEX CRIME	60 MONTHS

DURING THE TERM OF PRS, THE PERSON IS SUPERVISED BY A PROBATION/PAROLE OFFICER—THE SAME OFFICERS WHO SUPERVISE PROBATIONERS IN NORTH CAROLINA.

WHAT ABOUT MULTIPLE SENTENCES?

MANY INMATES ARE SERVING TIME FOR MORE THAN ONE CONVICTION.

BY DEFAULT, SENTENCES RUN **CONCURRENTLY.** THAT MEANS THE INMATE SERVES THEM ALL AT ONCE AND GETS RELEASED WHEN THE LONGEST SENTENCE IS COMPLETE.

A JUDGE CAN ORDER **CONSECUTIVE SENTENCES,** SOMETIMES CALLED "BOXCAR" SENTENCES. THAT MEANS ONE SENTENCE DOES NOT BEGIN UNTIL THE ONE BEFORE IT ENDS. THE PRISON SYSTEM COMBINES CONSECUTIVE SENTENCES INTO A SINGLE SENTENCE WITH **ONE POST-RELEASE SUPERVISION PERIOD** AT THE END.

THEY WILL ADD UP ALL THE CONFINEMENT PORTIONS AND THEN ELIMINATE ALL OF THE PRS PORTIONS EXCEPT FOR THE LONGEST ONE. FOR EXAMPLE, IF AN INMATE HAD A 20–36 MONTH SENTENCE FOR A CLASS E FELONY FOLLOWED BY TWO 6–17 MONTH CLASS H FELONY SENTENCES, IT WOULD LOOK LIKE THIS:

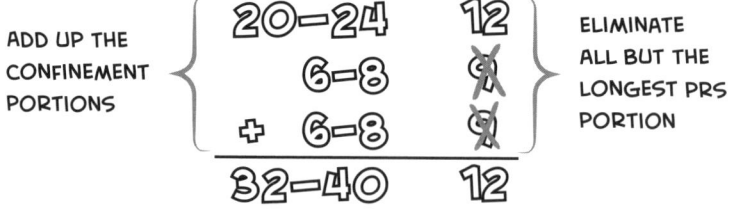

ADD UP THE CONFINEMENT PORTIONS

ELIMINATE ALL BUT THE LONGEST PRS PORTION

THE INMATE WILL SERVE BETWEEN 32 AND 40 MONTHS, DEPENDING ON EARNED TIME AND MERITORIOUS TIME, AND THEN BE RELEASED ONTO PRS FOR 12 MONTHS.

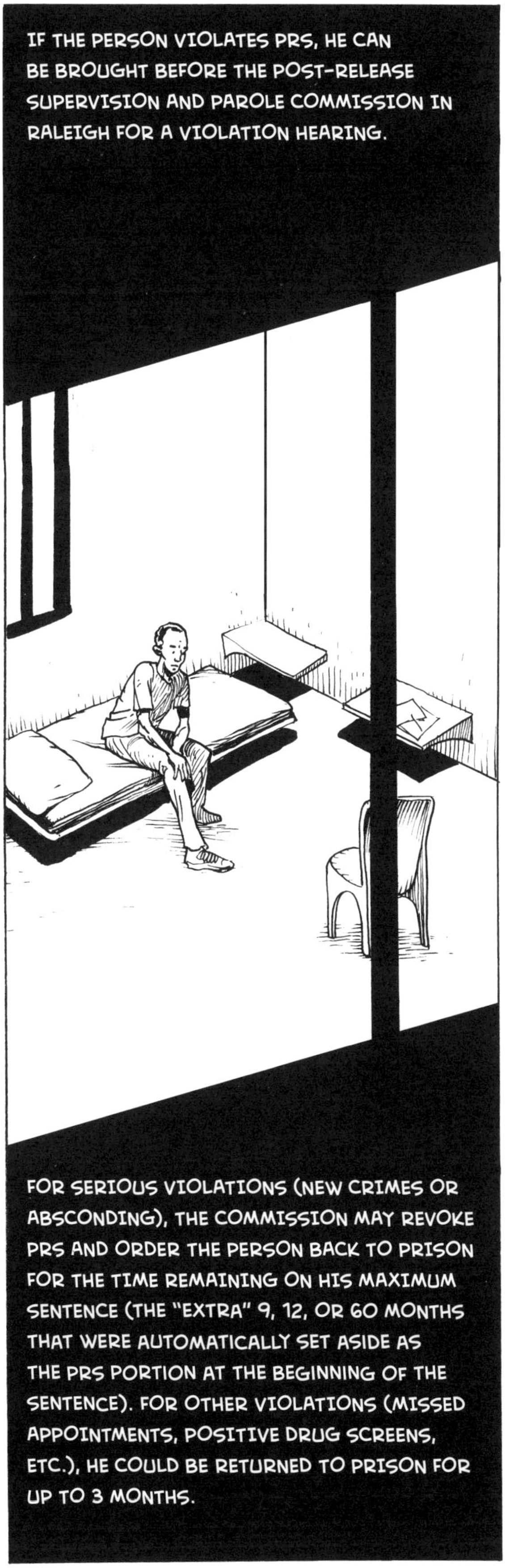

IF THE PERSON VIOLATES PRS, HE CAN BE BROUGHT BEFORE THE POST-RELEASE SUPERVISION AND PAROLE COMMISSION IN RALEIGH FOR A VIOLATION HEARING.

ONCE THE PRS PERIOD EXPIRES OR ALL THE TIME REMAINING ON THE REMAINING TERM OF IMPRISONMENT HAS BEEN SERVED, THE SENTENCE IS COMPLETE.

FOR SERIOUS VIOLATIONS (NEW CRIMES OR ABSCONDING), THE COMMISSION MAY REVOKE PRS AND ORDER THE PERSON BACK TO PRISON FOR THE TIME REMAINING ON HIS MAXIMUM SENTENCE (THE "EXTRA" 9, 12, OR 60 MONTHS THAT WERE AUTOMATICALLY SET ASIDE AS THE PRS PORTION AT THE BEGINNING OF THE SENTENCE). FOR OTHER VIOLATIONS (MISSED APPOINTMENTS, POSITIVE DRUG SCREENS, ETC.), HE COULD BE RETURNED TO PRISON FOR UP TO 3 MONTHS.

Jamie Markham is an associate professor of public law and government at the School of Government. He joined the faculty in 2007. His area of interest is criminal law and procedure, with a focus on the law of sentencing and corrections.

Shane Tharrington is the manager of classification and technical support for the prisons division of North Carolina's Department of Public Safety. He has worked in many capacities in the prison system for twenty-five years.

Jason Whitley is a painter, illustrator, and cartoonist. His portrait of Charlotte Hawkins Brown is in the Charlotte Hawkins Brown Museum. His newspaper comic strip, Sea Urchins, is collected into four books.

UNC
SCHOOL OF
GOVERNMENT

IN PRISON

9 781560 118992

ISBN-13: 978-1-56011-899-2
2017.04

This publication was printed and assembled by inmates and staff at the Correction Enterprises Print Plant.

CORRECTION
ENTERPRISES

Not Just Making It Right. Making It Better.

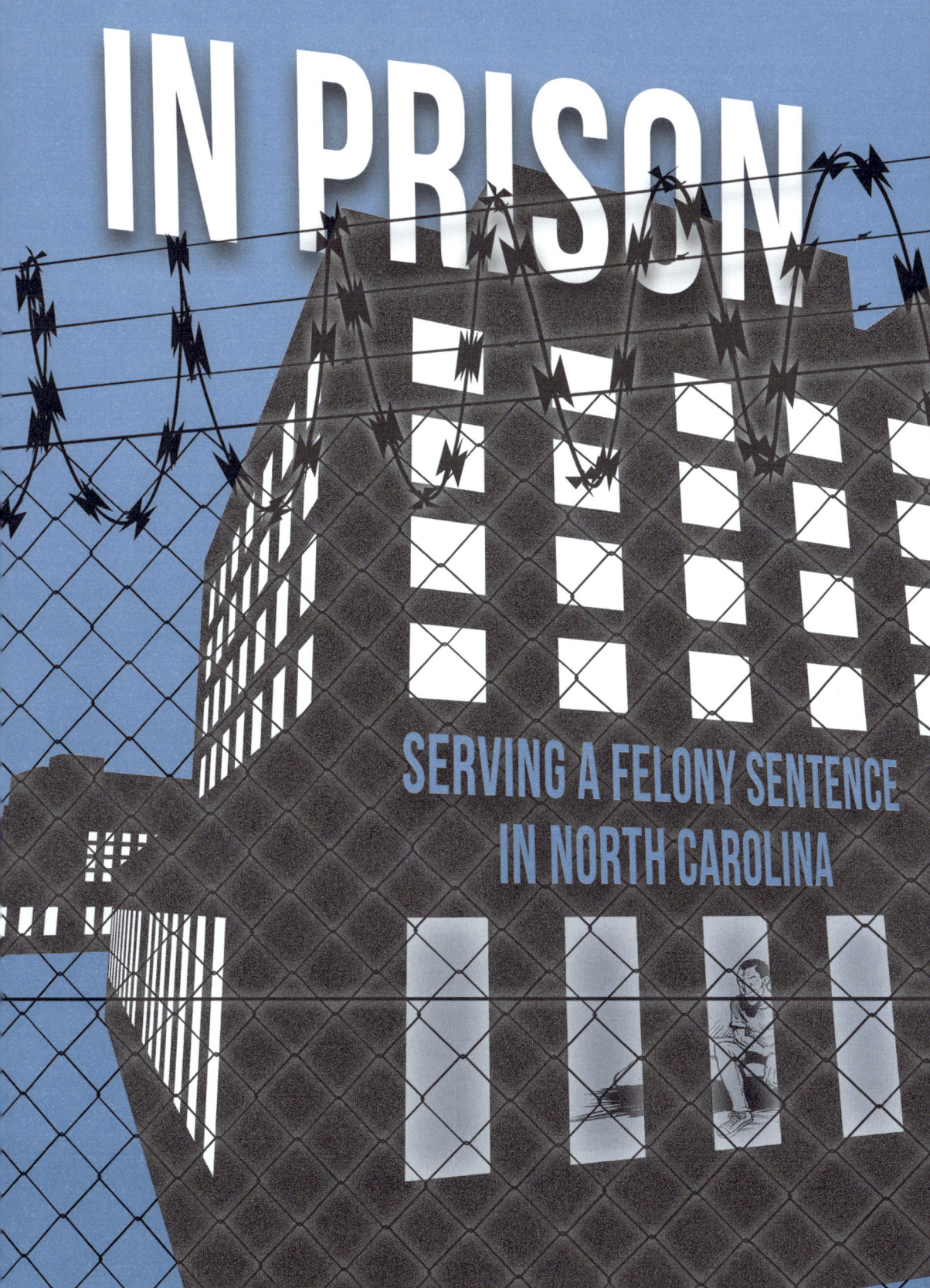

IN PRISON

SERVING A FELONY SENTENCE IN NORTH CAROLINA

MARKHAM
THARRINGTON
WHITLEY

The School of Government at the University of North Carolina at Chapel Hill works to improve the lives of North Carolinians by engaging in practical scholarship that helps public officials and citizens understand and improve state and local government. Established in 1931 as the Institute of Government, the School provides educational, advisory, and research services for state and local governments. The School of Government is also home to a nationally ranked Master of Public Administration program, the North Carolina Judicial College, and specialized centers focused on community and economic development, information technology, and environmental finance.

As the largest university-based local government training, advisory, and research organization in the United States, the School of Government offers up to 200 courses, webinars, and specialized conferences for more than 12,000 public officials each year. In addition, faculty members annually publish approximately 50 books, manuals, reports, articles, bulletins, and other print and online content related to state and local government. The School also produces the *Daily Bulletin Online* each day the General Assembly is in session, reporting on activities for members of the legislature and others who need to follow the course of legislation.

Operating support for the School of Government's programs and activities comes from many sources, including state appropriations, local government membership dues, private contributions, publication sales, course fees, and service contracts.

Visit sog.unc.edu or call 919.966.5381 for more information on the School's courses, publications, programs, and services.

© 2017
School of Government
The University of North Carolina at Chapel Hill

Printed in the United States of America

21 20 19 18 17   1 2 3 4 5

ISBN 978-1-56011-899-2

♾ This publication is printed on permanent, acid-free paper in compliance with the North Carolina General Statutes.

♻ Printed on recycled paper

INTRODUCTION

This short book explains how a felony prison sentence is served in North Carolina. I hope those who read it will gain a better sense of where and how an inmate serves his or her time.

Presenting the information in illustrated form is by no means intended to make light of a very serious subject. It is, rather, offered as an accessible way to fill gaps in knowledge and to address common misperceptions about the way sentences are served. It is meant to give crime victims, defendants, inmates, and their families an understandable resource that translates the words and numbers on a sentencing judgment into a practical reality.

Though the book is of course not a comprehensive legal reference, I hope it will be useful to lawyers and judges, too. An improved understanding of how a sentence is administered should help you advise your clients, negotiate your pleas, and craft your judgments in a way that achieves a more refined measure of justice in each case.

I have neither the technical expertise nor the artistic talent to create something like this on my own. For the former, I relied on co-author Shane Tharrington, classification manager for North Carolina's Division of Adult Correction. For the latter, I turned to Jason Whitley, a talented illustrator who works as a creative lead for instructional innovation at the Eshelman School of Pharmacy at UNC-Chapel Hill. Many thanks to Shane (and to the prison system as a whole) for answering my many questions, and to Jason for turning my stick-figure storyboard into a real graphic novel.

Jamie Markham
Chapel Hill
September 2017

THE DEFENDANT WILL BE HELD IN THE COUNTY JAIL UNTIL THE PRISON SYSTEM PICKS HIM UP, USUALLY WITHIN A WEEK OR SO.

IF THE DEFENDANT APPEALS HIS SENTENCE, HE COULD BE RELEASED ON AN APPEAL BOND, BUT THAT IS RARE.

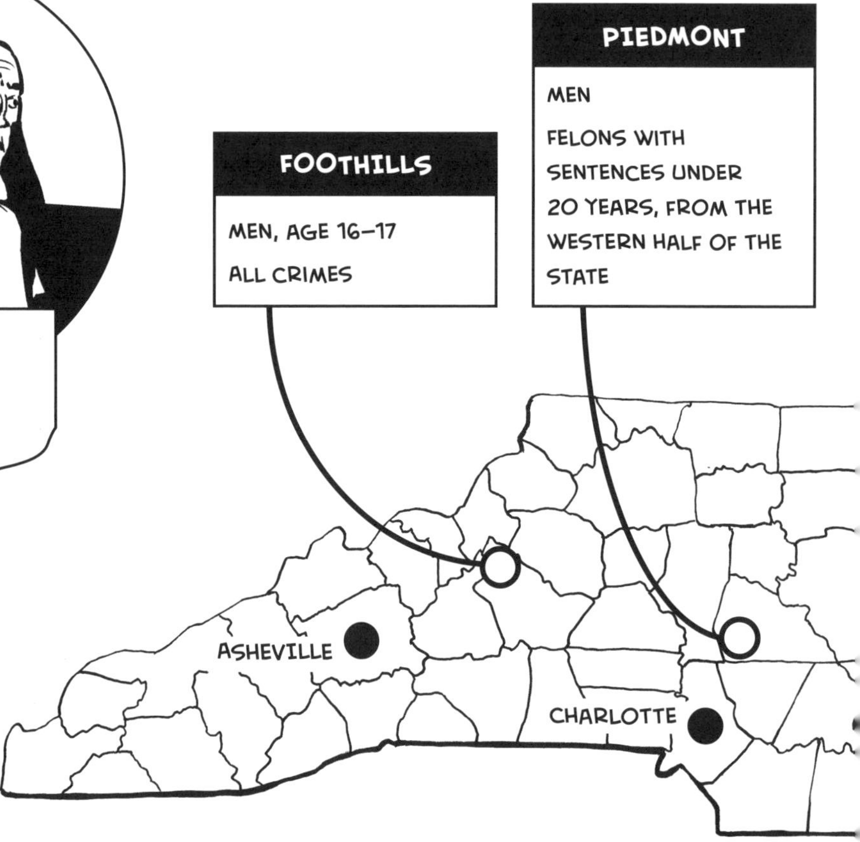

THE DEFENDANT'S FIRST STOP WILL BE ONE OF NORTH CAROLINA'S DIAGNOSTIC CENTERS.

FOOTHILLS

MEN, AGE 16–17

ALL CRIMES

PIEDMONT

MEN

FELONS WITH SENTENCES UNDER 20 YEARS, FROM THE WESTERN HALF OF THE STATE

ASHEVILLE

CHARLOTTE

NORTH CAROLINA'S DIAGNOSTIC CENTERS

THE DEFENDANT GENERALLY WILL GET JAIL CREDIT FOR ALL THE DAYS HE SPENT IN JAIL BEFORE CONVICTION.

JAIL CREDIT IS SUBTRACTED FROM BOTH THE MINIMUM AND MAXIMUM SENTENCE. FOR EXAMPLE, IF THE DEFENDANT HAD 2 MONTHS OF JAIL CREDIT, HE WOULD HAVE 8–19 MONTHS LEFT TO SERVE OF HIS 10–21 MONTH SENTENCE.

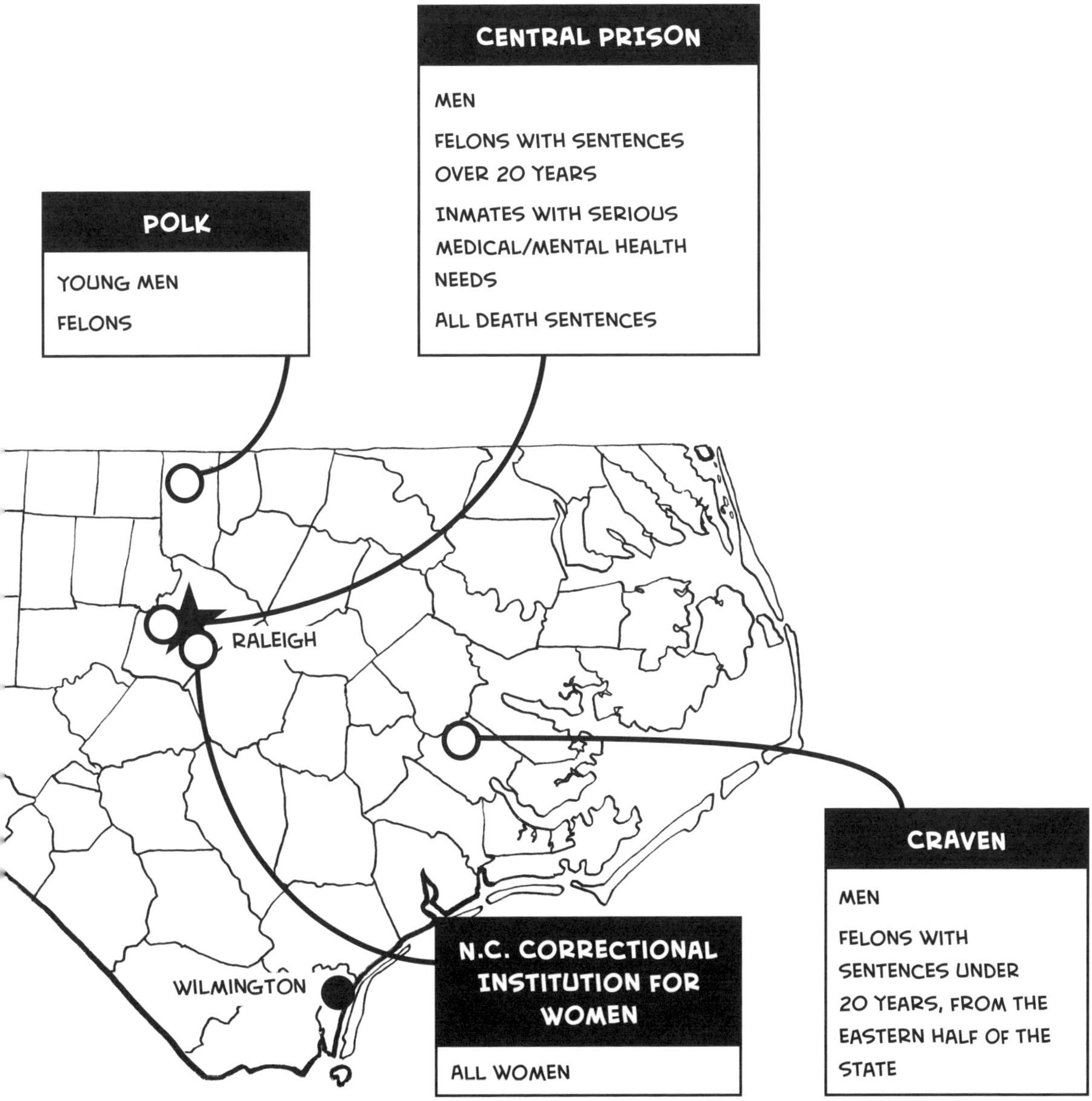

CENTRAL PRISON

MEN

FELONS WITH SENTENCES OVER 20 YEARS

INMATES WITH SERIOUS MEDICAL/MENTAL HEALTH NEEDS

ALL DEATH SENTENCES

POLK

YOUNG MEN

FELONS

RALEIGH

WILMINGTON

CRAVEN

MEN

FELONS WITH SENTENCES UNDER 20 YEARS, FROM THE EASTERN HALF OF THE STATE

N.C. CORRECTIONAL INSTITUTION FOR WOMEN

ALL WOMEN

THE DEFENDANT WILL SPEND 2-4 WEEKS AT THE DIAGNOSTIC FACILITY COMPLETING VARIOUS INPROCESSING ACTIVITES.

CLOTHING EXCHANGE

FINGERPRINTING

RISK-NEEDS ASSESSMENT

DNA SAMPLE

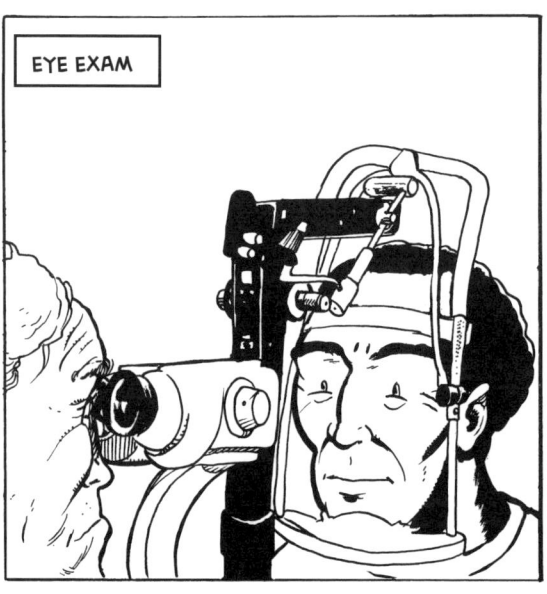

EYE EXAM

INTELLIGENCE TESTING

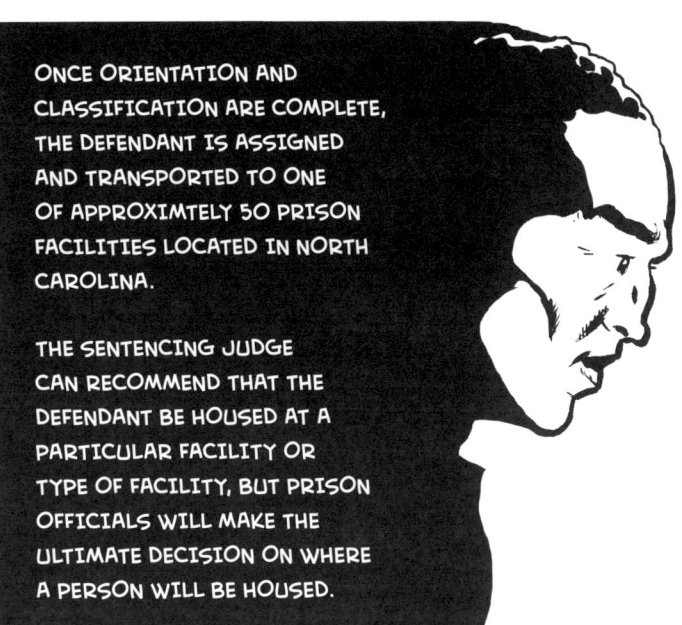

ONCE ORIENTATION AND CLASSIFICATION ARE COMPLETE, THE DEFENDANT IS ASSIGNED AND TRANSPORTED TO ONE OF APPROXIMTELY 50 PRISON FACILITIES LOCATED IN NORTH CAROLINA.

THE SENTENCING JUDGE CAN RECOMMEND THAT THE DEFENDANT BE HOUSED AT A PARTICULAR FACILITY OR TYPE OF FACILITY, BUT PRISON OFFICIALS WILL MAKE THE ULTIMATE DECISION ON WHERE A PERSON WILL BE HOUSED.

THE HOUSING DECISION IS BASED IN PART ON THE CUSTODY LEVEL TO WHICH THE INMATE IS ASSIGNED DURING CLASSIFICATION.

THERE ARE THREE MAIN CUSTODY LEVELS IN THE NORTH CAROLINA PRISON SYSTEM:

CLOSE CUSTODY (MOST SECURE)

MEDIUM CUSTODY

MINIMUM CUSTODY

THE MAP BELOW SHOWS SOME OF THE PRISONS TO WHICH AN INMATE MIGHT BE ASSIGNED. IT HIGHLIGHTS A SAMPLING OF THE SPECIAL PROGRAMS AND JOB ASSIGNMENTS AVAILABLE AT CERTAIN PRISONS. OVER THE COURSE OF SERVING A SENTENCE, SOME INMATES WILL TRANSFER BETWEEN FACILITIES AS CUSTODY LEVELS, WORK ASSIGNMENTS, AND PROGRAM NEEDS CHANGE.

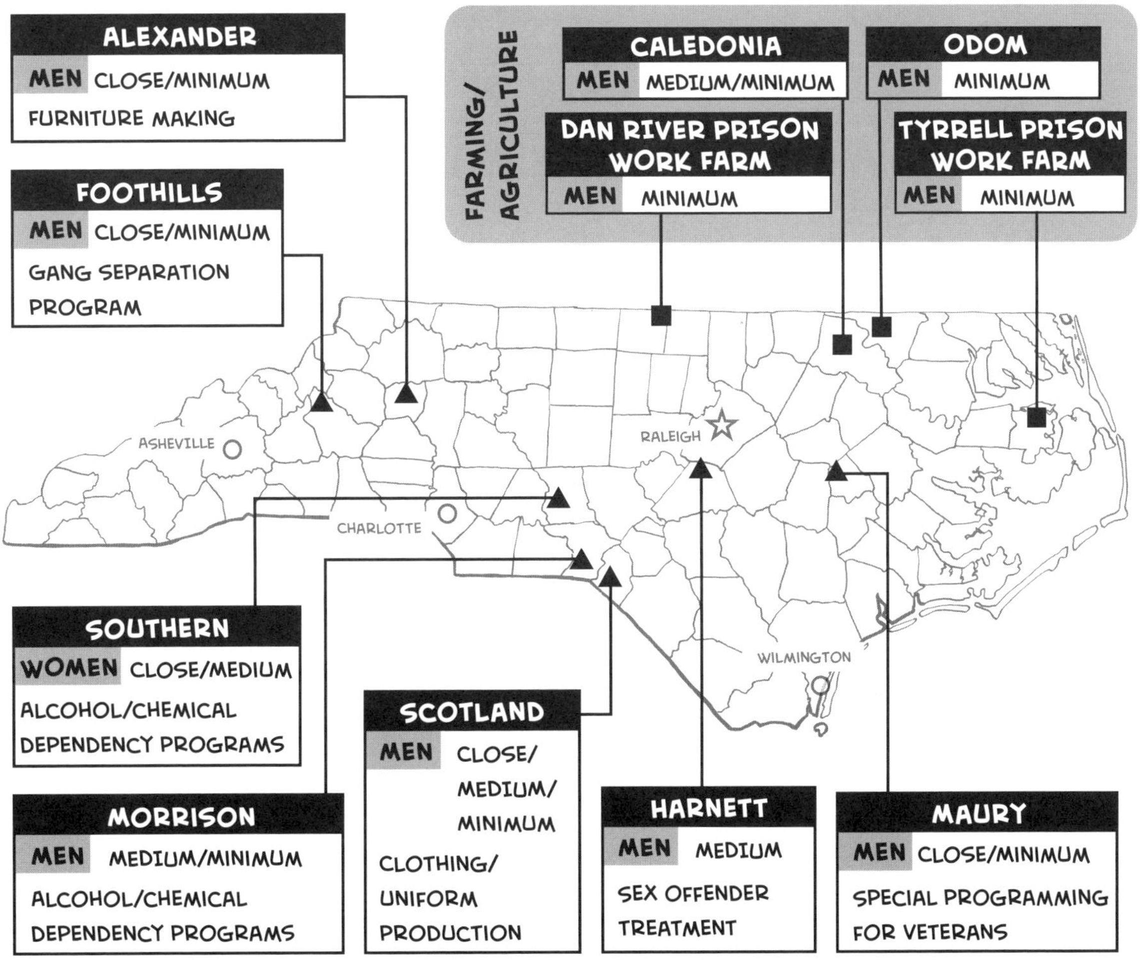

ALEXANDER
MEN CLOSE/MINIMUM
FURNITURE MAKING

FOOTHILLS
MEN CLOSE/MINIMUM
GANG SEPARATION PROGRAM

FARMING/AGRICULTURE

CALEDONIA
MEN MEDIUM/MINIMUM

DAN RIVER PRISON WORK FARM
MEN MINIMUM

ODOM
MEN MINIMUM

TYRRELL PRISON WORK FARM
MEN MINIMUM

ASHEVILLE
RALEIGH
CHARLOTTE
WILMINGTON

SOUTHERN
WOMEN CLOSE/MEDIUM
ALCOHOL/CHEMICAL DEPENDENCY PROGRAMS

SCOTLAND
MEN CLOSE/MEDIUM/MINIMUM
CLOTHING/UNIFORM PRODUCTION

MORRISON
MEN MEDIUM/MINIMUM
ALCOHOL/CHEMICAL DEPENDENCY PROGRAMS

HARNETT
MEN MEDIUM
SEX OFFENDER TREATMENT

MAURY
MEN CLOSE/MINIMUM
SPECIAL PROGRAMMING FOR VETERANS

AT THE ASSIGNED FACLITY, THE INMATE BEGINS SERVING THE REMAINDER OF HIS SENTENCE. HOW LONG IT WILL TAKE TO SERVE IT DEPENDS IN PART ON WHAT HE DOES IN PRISON. PARTICIPATION IN WORK AND PROGRAMS ALLOWS AN INMATE TO EARN SENTENCE CREDITS CALLED **EARNED TIME.**

EARNED TIME IS AWARDED AT DIFFERENT RATES DEPENDING ON THE TYPE OF WORK OR PROGRAM COMPLETED. IN GENERAL, PARTICIPATION IN ANY OF THE JOBS OR PROGRAMS SHOWN BELOW WOULD BE REWARDED WITH 9 DAYS OF EARNED TIME PER MONTH.

EDUCATIONAL PROGRAMS

LAUNDRY

LICENSE PLATES

CONSTRUCTION

CUSTODIAL WORK

AN INMATE AWAITING A WORK
OR PROGRAM ASSIGNMENT
GENERALLY GETS 3 DAYS
OF EARNED TIME
PER MONTH.

INMATES CAN ALSO GET ANOTHER
CREDIT CALLED **MERITORIOUS TIME**
FOR EXEMPLARY ACTS, LIKE WORKING
IN BAD WEATHER OR
COMPLETING AN
EDUCATIONAL DEGREE.

WELDING

ROAD
SIGNS

TREATMENT GROUP

DOG TRAINING

ROAD
WORK

KITCHEN
WORK

SO WHEN IS AN INMATE RELEASED?

FELONY ACTIVE SENTENCES HAVE TWO PARTS: A PERIOD OF CONFINEMENT IN PRISON, FOLLOWED BY A PERIOD OF **POST-RELEASE SUPERVISION** (PRS). PRS IS A PERIOD OF SUPERVISED RELEASE IN THE COMMUNITY, SIMILAR TO PROBATION.

THE LENGTH OF THE PRS PORTION OF THE SENTENCE DEPENDS ON THE INMATE'S CLASS OF OFFENSE AND WHETHER OR NOT THE CRIME REQUIRES REGISTRATION AS A SEX OFFENDER.

OFFENSE CLASS	PRS PORTION OF MAXIMUM
CLASS F-I	9 MONTHS
CLASS B1-E	12 MONTHS
CLASS B1-E SEX CRIME	60 MONTHS

THE PRISON SYSTEM AUTOMATICALLY SUBTRACTS THE PRS PORTION OF THE SENTENCE FROM THE MAXIMUM AND SETS IT OFF TO THE SIDE. THAT'S BECAUSE THE INMATE WILL SERVE THAT TIME ONLY IF HIS POST-RELEASE SUPERVISION IS REVOKED. THE TIME THAT REMAINS AFTER SUBTRACTING THE PRS PORTION IS THE CONFINEMENT PORTION OF THE SENTENCE—THE TIME THE PERSON WILL ACTUALLY SPEND IN PRISON.

↓ MAXIMUM SENTENCE ↓

SOME PEOPLE THINK ALL INMATES ARE RELEASED ONCE THEY HAVE SERVED THEIR MINIMUM SENTENCE. **THEY AREN'T**. INSTEAD, THE INMATE STARTS FROM THE MAXIMUM AND WORKS HIS WAY DOWN THROUGH EARNED TIME AND MERITORIOUS TIME.

MINIMUM SENTENCE

THE MINIMUM SENTENCE IS JUST THE LOWER LIMIT ON HOW MUCH THE SENTENCE MAY BE REDUCED. IN OTHER WORDS, NO MATTER HOW MUCH WORK HE DOES OR HOW MANY PROGRAMS HE COMPLETES, THE INMATE WILL NOT BE RELEASED BEFORE SERVING HIS MINIMUM SENTENCE.

MOST INMATES ARE NOT ABLE TO WORK THEIR SENTENCES ALL THE WAY DOWN TO THE MINIMUM. AVERAGE RELEASE DATES FOR EACH CLASS OF FELONY ARE SHOWN IN THE TABLE BELOW.

OFFENSE CLASS	PERCENT OF MINIMUM SERVED UPON RELEASE...
CLASS B1–C	102%
CLASS D	103%
CLASS E	104%
CLASS F	105%
CLASS G	107%
CLASS H	114%
CLASS I	113%

NOTICE THAT INMATES WITH MORE SERIOUS CONVICTIONS GENERALLY DO A BETTER JOB OF WORKING THEIR RELEASE DATES DOWN TOWARD THE MINIMUM SENTENCE. WHY? IT'S BECAUSE MANY INMATES WITH SHORTER SENTENCES AREN'T IN PRISON LONG ENOUGH TO COMPLETE PROGRAMS OR GET PLACED IN THE JOBS THAT EARN A LOT OF EARNED TIME.

LET'S PUT IT ALL TOGETHER FOR OUR EXAMPLE OF AN INMATE SERVING A 10–21 MONTH SENTENCE FOR A CLASS G FELONY. THE LAST 9 MONTHS OF HIS SENTENCE WILL BE SET ASIDE FOR PRS, LEAVING 10–12 MONTHS OF CONFINEMENT TO SERVE. ON AVERAGE, AN INMATE WITH A SENTENCE LIKE THAT WILL SERVE 107% OF HIS MINIMUM (10.7 MONTHS IN THIS CASE) BEFORE BEING RELEASED ONTO PRS. THE EARLIEST POSSIBLE RELEASE IS 10 MONTHS. THE LATEST IS 12 MONTHS.

10–12 MONTHS

CONFINEMENT PORTION

9 MONTHS

PRS PORTION

A FELONY INMATE'S SENTENCE IS NOT COMPLETE UPON RELEASE. ALL FELONS SERVE A TERM OF POST-RELEASE SUPERVISION (PRS) AFTER THEY ARE RELEASED FROM PRISON. IT'S MANDATORY—THE INMATE CANNOT REFUSE IT. THE LENGTH OF THE PRS TERM IS GOVERNED BY THE TYPE OF SENTENCE.

OFFENSE CLASS	LENGTH OF PRS
CLASS F—I	9 MONTHS
CLASS B1—E	12 MONTHS
SEX CRIME	60 MONTHS

DURING THE TERM OF PRS, THE PERSON IS SUPERVISED BY A PROBATION/PAROLE OFFICER—THE SAME OFFICERS WHO SUPERVISE PROBATIONERS IN NORTH CAROLINA.

WHAT ABOUT MULTIPLE SENTENCES?

MANY INMATES ARE SERVING TIME FOR MORE THAN ONE CONVICTION.

BY DEFAULT, SENTENCES RUN **CONCURRENTLY.** THAT MEANS THE INMATE SERVES THEM ALL AT ONCE AND GETS RELEASED WHEN THE LONGEST SENTENCE IS COMPLETE.

A JUDGE CAN ORDER **CONSECUTIVE SENTENCES,** SOMETIMES CALLED "BOXCAR" SENTENCES. THAT MEANS ONE SENTENCE DOES NOT BEGIN UNTIL THE ONE BEFORE IT ENDS. THE PRISON SYSTEM COMBINES CONSECUTIVE SENTENCES INTO A SINGLE SENTENCE WITH **ONE POST-RELEASE SUPERVISION PERIOD** AT THE END.

THEY WILL ADD UP ALL THE CONFINEMENT PORTIONS AND THEN ELIMINATE ALL OF THE PRS PORTIONS EXCEPT FOR THE LONGEST ONE. FOR EXAMPLE, IF AN INMATE HAD A 20—36 MONTH SENTENCE FOR A CLASS E FELONY FOLLOWED BY TWO 6—17 MONTH CLASS H FELONY SENTENCES, IT WOULD LOOK LIKE THIS:

ADD UP THE CONFINEMENT PORTIONS

$$
\begin{array}{rl}
20-24 & 12 \\
6-8 & \cancel{9} \\
+\ 6-8 & \cancel{9} \\
\hline
32-40 & 12
\end{array}
$$

ELIMINATE ALL BUT THE LONGEST PRS PORTION

THE INMATE WILL SERVE BETWEEN 32 AND 40 MONTHS, DEPENDING ON EARNED TIME AND MERITORIOUS TIME, AND THEN BE RELEASED ONTO PRS FOR 12 MONTHS.

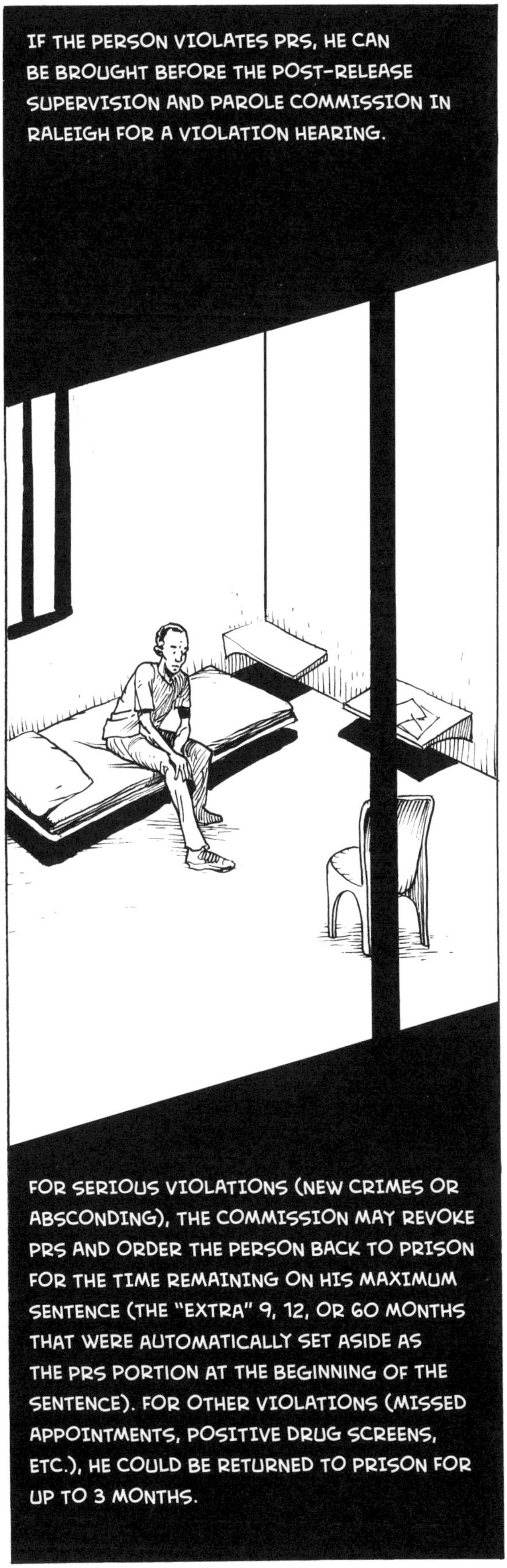

IF THE PERSON VIOLATES PRS, HE CAN BE BROUGHT BEFORE THE POST–RELEASE SUPERVISION AND PAROLE COMMISSION IN RALEIGH FOR A VIOLATION HEARING.

FOR SERIOUS VIOLATIONS (NEW CRIMES OR ABSCONDING), THE COMMISSION MAY REVOKE PRS AND ORDER THE PERSON BACK TO PRISON FOR THE TIME REMAINING ON HIS MAXIMUM SENTENCE (THE "EXTRA" 9, 12, OR 60 MONTHS THAT WERE AUTOMATICALLY SET ASIDE AS THE PRS PORTION AT THE BEGINNING OF THE SENTENCE). FOR OTHER VIOLATIONS (MISSED APPOINTMENTS, POSITIVE DRUG SCREENS, ETC.), HE COULD BE RETURNED TO PRISON FOR UP TO 3 MONTHS.

ONCE THE PRS PERIOD EXPIRES OR ALL THE TIME REMAINING ON THE REMAINING TERM OF IMPRISONMENT HAS BEEN SERVED, THE SENTENCE IS COMPLETE.

Jamie Markham is an associate professor of public law and government at the School of Government. He joined the faculty in 2007. His area of interest is criminal law and procedure, with a focus on the law of sentencing and corrections.

Shane Tharrington is the manager of classification and technical support for the prisons division of North Carolina's Department of Public Safety. He has worked in many capacities in the prison system for twenty-five years.

Jason Whitley is a painter, illustrator, and cartoonist. His portrait of Charlotte Hawkins Brown is in the Charlotte Hawkins Brown Museum. His newspaper comic strip, Sea Urchins, is collected into four books.

UNC
SCHOOL OF
GOVERNMENT

This publication was printed and assembled by inmates and staff at the Correction Enterprises Print Plant.

CORRECTION
ENTERPRISES

Not Just Making It Right. Making It Better.

ISBN-13: 978-1-56011-899-2

2017.04

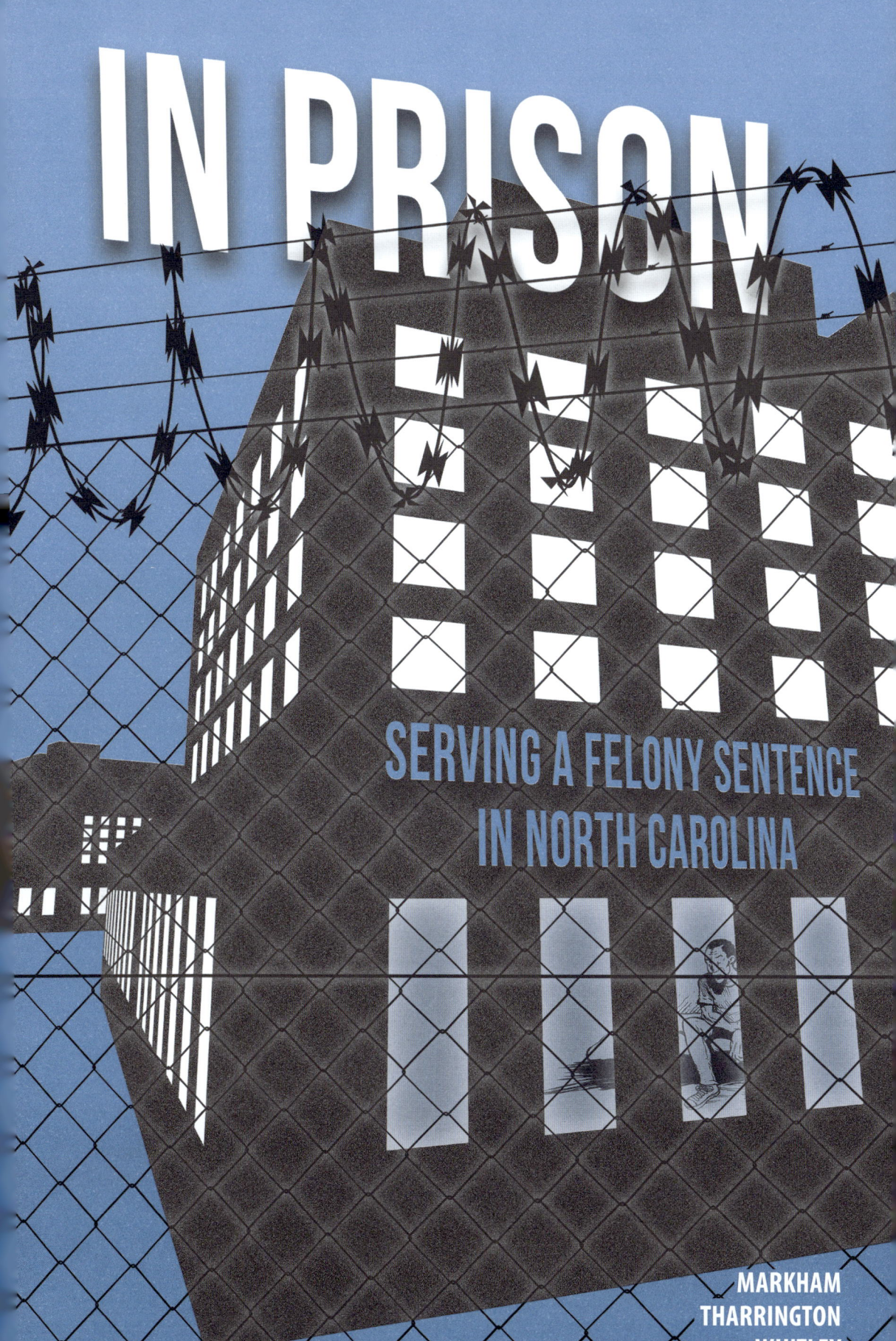

IN PRISON

SERVING A FELONY SENTENCE IN NORTH CAROLINA

MARKHAM
THARRINGTON
WHITLEY

The School of Government at the University of North Carolina at Chapel Hill works to improve the lives of North Carolinians by engaging in practical scholarship that helps public officials and citizens understand and improve state and local government. Established in 1931 as the Institute of Government, the School provides educational, advisory, and research services for state and local governments. The School of Government is also home to a nationally ranked Master of Public Administration program, the North Carolina Judicial College, and specialized centers focused on community and economic development, information technology, and environmental finance.

As the largest university-based local government training, advisory, and research organization in the United States, the School of Government offers up to 200 courses, webinars, and specialized conferences for more than 12,000 public officials each year. In addition, faculty members annually publish approximately 50 books, manuals, reports, articles, bulletins, and other print and online content related to state and local government. The School also produces the *Daily Bulletin Online* each day the General Assembly is in session, reporting on activities for members of the legislature and others who need to follow the course of legislation.

Operating support for the School of Government's programs and activities comes from many sources, including state appropriations, local government membership dues, private contributions, publication sales, course fees, and service contracts.

Visit sog.unc.edu or call 919.966.5381 for more information on the School's courses, publications, programs, and services.

© 2017
School of Government
The University of North Carolina at Chapel Hill

Printed in the United States of America

21 20 19 18 17   1 2 3 4 5

ISBN 978-1-56011-899-2

∞ This publication is printed on permanent, acid-free paper in compliance with the North Carolina General Statutes.

♻ Printed on recycled paper

INTRODUCTION

This short book explains how a felony prison sentence is served in North Carolina. I hope those who read it will gain a better sense of where and how an inmate serves his or her time.

Presenting the information in illustrated form is by no means intended to make light of a very serious subject. It is, rather, offered as an accessible way to fill gaps in knowledge and to address common misperceptions about the way sentences are served. It is meant to give crime victims, defendants, inmates, and their families an understandable resource that translates the words and numbers on a sentencing judgment into a practical reality.

Though the book is of course not a comprehensive legal reference, I hope it will be useful to lawyers and judges, too. An improved understanding of how a sentence is administered should help you advise your clients, negotiate your pleas, and craft your judgments in a way that achieves a more refined measure of justice in each case.

I have neither the technical expertise nor the artistic talent to create something like this on my own. For the former, I relied on co-author Shane Tharrington, classification manager for North Carolina's Division of Adult Correction. For the latter, I turned to Jason Whitley, a talented illustrator who works as a creative lead for instructional innovation at the Eshelman School of Pharmacy at UNC-Chapel Hill. Many thanks to Shane (and to the prison system as a whole) for answering my many questions, and to Jason for turning my stick-figure storyboard into a real graphic novel.

Jamie Markham
Chapel Hill
September 2017

THE DEFENDANT WILL BE HELD IN THE COUNTY JAIL UNTIL THE PRISON SYSTEM PICKS HIM UP, USUALLY WITHIN A WEEK OR SO.

IF THE DEFENDANT APPEALS HIS SENTENCE, HE COULD BE RELEASED ON AN APPEAL BOND, BUT THAT IS RARE.

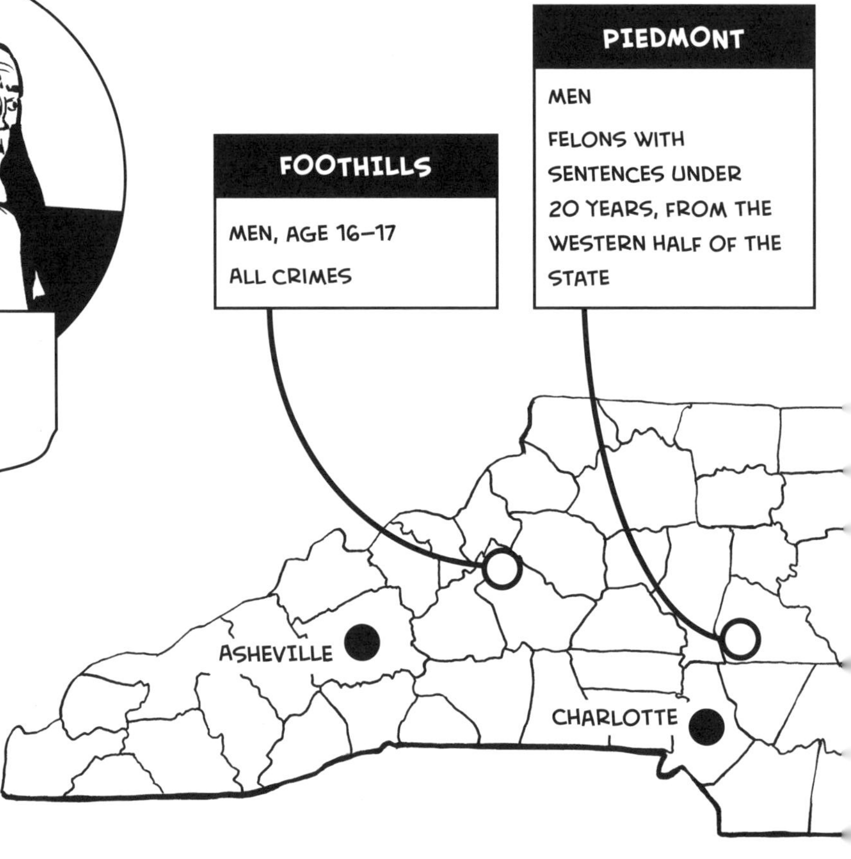

THE DEFENDANT'S FIRST STOP WILL BE ONE OF NORTH CAROLINA'S DIAGNOSTIC CENTERS.

FOOTHILLS

MEN, AGE 16–17
ALL CRIMES

PIEDMONT

MEN

FELONS WITH SENTENCES UNDER 20 YEARS, FROM THE WESTERN HALF OF THE STATE

ASHEVILLE

CHARLOTTE

NORTH CAROLINA'S DIAGNOSTIC CENTERS

THE DEFENDANT GENERALLY WILL GET JAIL CREDIT FOR ALL THE DAYS HE SPENT IN JAIL BEFORE CONVICTION.

JAIL CREDIT IS SUBTRACTED FROM BOTH THE MINIMUM AND MAXIMUM SENTENCE. FOR EXAMPLE, IF THE DEFENDANT HAD 2 MONTHS OF JAIL CREDIT, HE WOULD HAVE 8–19 MONTHS LEFT TO SERVE OF HIS 10–21 MONTH SENTENCE.

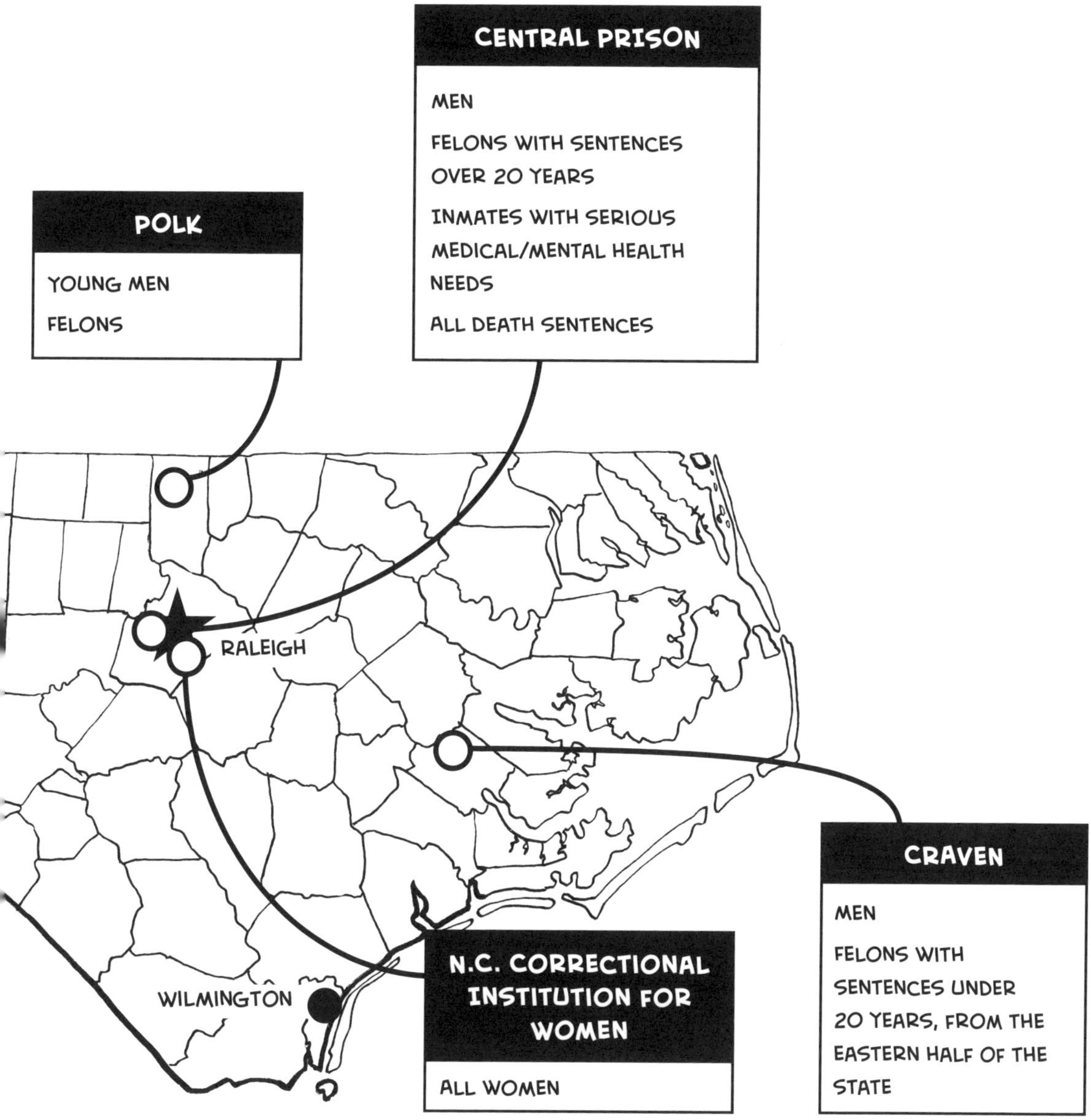

CENTRAL PRISON

MEN

FELONS WITH SENTENCES OVER 20 YEARS

INMATES WITH SERIOUS MEDICAL/MENTAL HEALTH NEEDS

ALL DEATH SENTENCES

POLK

YOUNG MEN

FELONS

RALEIGH

WILMINGTON

N.C. CORRECTIONAL INSTITUTION FOR WOMEN

ALL WOMEN

CRAVEN

MEN

FELONS WITH SENTENCES UNDER 20 YEARS, FROM THE EASTERN HALF OF THE STATE

THE DEFENDANT WILL SPEND 2-4 WEEKS AT THE DIAGNOSTIC FACILITY COMPLETING VARIOUS INPROCESSING ACTIVITES.

CLOTHING EXCHANGE

FINGERPRINTING

RISK-NEEDS ASSESSMENT

DNA SAMPLE

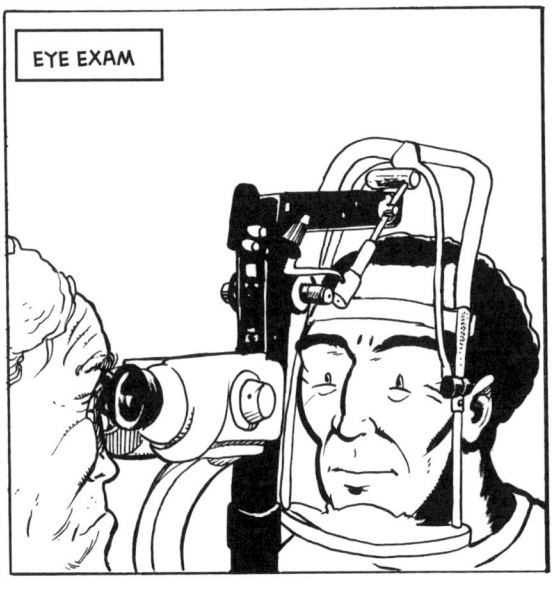

EYE EXAM

INTELLIGENCE TESTING

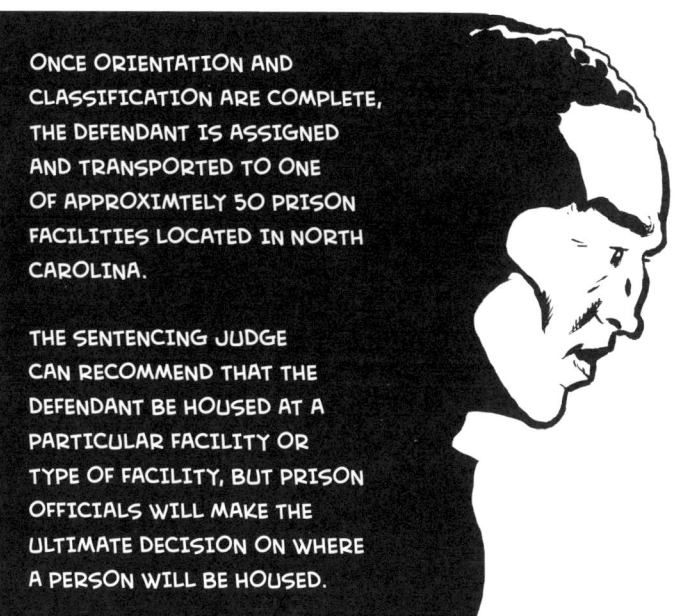

ONCE ORIENTATION AND CLASSIFICATION ARE COMPLETE, THE DEFENDANT IS ASSIGNED AND TRANSPORTED TO ONE OF APPROXIMTELY 50 PRISON FACILITIES LOCATED IN NORTH CAROLINA.

THE SENTENCING JUDGE CAN RECOMMEND THAT THE DEFENDANT BE HOUSED AT A PARTICULAR FACILITY OR TYPE OF FACILITY, BUT PRISON OFFICIALS WILL MAKE THE ULTIMATE DECISION ON WHERE A PERSON WILL BE HOUSED.

THE HOUSING DECISION IS BASED IN PART ON THE CUSTODY LEVEL TO WHICH THE INMATE IS ASSIGNED DURING CLASSIFICATION.

THERE ARE THREE MAIN CUSTODY LEVELS IN THE NORTH CAROLINA PRISON SYSTEM:

CLOSE CUSTODY (MOST SECURE)

MEDIUM CUSTODY

MINIMUM CUSTODY

THE MAP BELOW SHOWS SOME OF THE PRISONS TO WHICH AN INMATE MIGHT BE ASSIGNED. IT HIGHLIGHTS A SAMPLING OF THE SPECIAL PROGRAMS AND JOB ASSIGNMENTS AVAILABLE AT CERTAIN PRISONS. OVER THE COURSE OF SERVING A SENTENCE, SOME INMATES WILL TRANSFER BETWEEN FACILITIES AS CUSTODY LEVELS, WORK ASSIGNMENTS, AND PROGRAM NEEDS CHANGE.

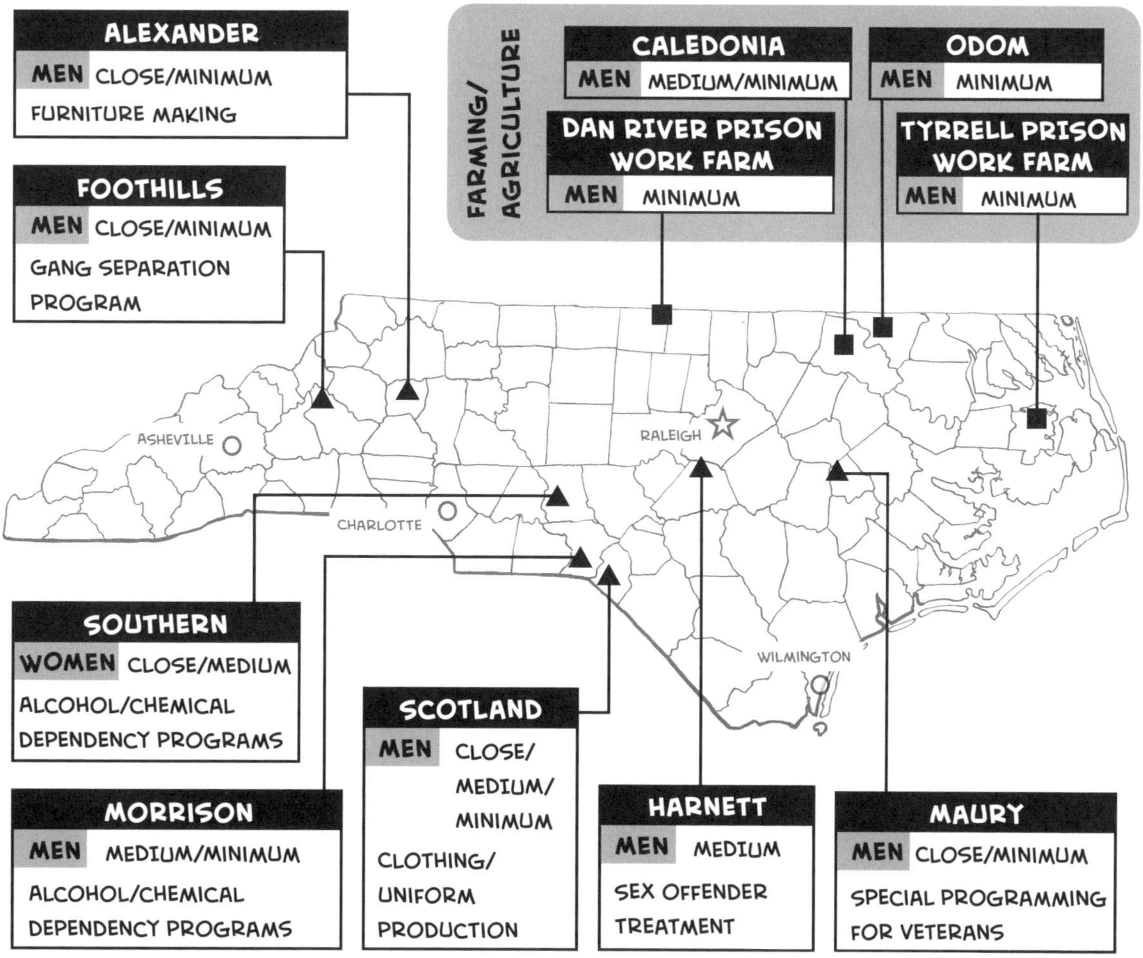

ALEXANDER
MEN CLOSE/MINIMUM
FURNITURE MAKING

FOOTHILLS
MEN CLOSE/MINIMUM
GANG SEPARATION PROGRAM

FARMING/AGRICULTURE

CALEDONIA
MEN MEDIUM/MINIMUM

DAN RIVER PRISON WORK FARM
MEN MINIMUM

ODOM
MEN MINIMUM

TYRRELL PRISON WORK FARM
MEN MINIMUM

ASHEVILLE

RALEIGH

CHARLOTTE

WILMINGTON

SOUTHERN
WOMEN CLOSE/MEDIUM
ALCOHOL/CHEMICAL DEPENDENCY PROGRAMS

MORRISON
MEN MEDIUM/MINIMUM
ALCOHOL/CHEMICAL DEPENDENCY PROGRAMS

SCOTLAND
MEN CLOSE/MEDIUM/MINIMUM
CLOTHING/UNIFORM PRODUCTION

HARNETT
MEN MEDIUM
SEX OFFENDER TREATMENT

MAURY
MEN CLOSE/MINIMUM
SPECIAL PROGRAMMING FOR VETERANS

AT THE ASSIGNED FACLITY, THE INMATE BEGINS SERVING THE REMAINDER OF HIS SENTENCE. HOW LONG IT WILL TAKE TO SERVE IT DEPENDS IN PART ON WHAT HE DOES IN PRISON. PARTICIPATION IN WORK AND PROGRAMS ALLOWS AN INMATE TO EARN SENTENCE CREDITS CALLED **EARNED TIME**.

EARNED TIME IS AWARDED AT DIFFERENT RATES DEPENDING ON THE TYPE OF WORK OR PROGRAM COMPLETED. IN GENERAL, PARTICIPATION IN ANY OF THE JOBS OR PROGRAMS SHOWN BELOW WOULD BE REWARDED WITH 9 DAYS OF EARNED TIME PER MONTH.

EDUCATIONAL PROGRAMS

LAUNDRY

LICENSE PLATES

CONSTRUCTION

CUSTODIAL WORK

AN INMATE AWAITING A WORK OR PROGRAM ASSIGNMENT GENERALLY GETS 3 DAYS OF EARNED TIME PER MONTH.

INMATES CAN ALSO GET ANOTHER CREDIT CALLED **MERITORIOUS TIME** FOR EXEMPLARY ACTS, LIKE WORKING IN BAD WEATHER OR COMPLETING AN EDUCATIONAL DEGREE.

WELDING

ROAD SIGNS

TREATMENT GROUP

DOG TRAINING

ROAD WORK

KITCHEN WORK

SO WHEN IS AN INMATE RELEASED?

FELONY ACTIVE SENTENCES HAVE TWO PARTS: A PERIOD OF CONFINEMENT IN PRISON, FOLLOWED BY A PERIOD OF **POST-RELEASE SUPERVISION** (PRS). PRS IS A PERIOD OF SUPERVISED RELEASE IN THE COMMUNITY, SIMILAR TO PROBATION.

THE LENGTH OF THE PRS PORTION OF THE SENTENCE DEPENDS ON THE INMATE'S CLASS OF OFFENSE AND WHETHER OR NOT THE CRIME REQUIRES REGISTRATION AS A SEX OFFENDER.

OFFENSE CLASS	PRS PORTION OF MAXIMUM
CLASS F-I	9 MONTHS
CLASS B1-E	12 MONTHS
CLASS B1-E SEX CRIME	60 MONTHS

THE PRISON SYSTEM AUTOMATICALLY SUBTRACTS THE PRS PORTION OF THE SENTENCE FROM THE MAXIMUM AND SETS IT OFF TO THE SIDE. THAT'S BECAUSE THE INMATE WILL SERVE THAT TIME ONLY IF HIS POST-RELEASE SUPERVISION IS REVOKED. THE TIME THAT REMAINS AFTER SUBTRACTING THE PRS PORTION IS THE CONFINEMENT PORTION OF THE SENTENCE—THE TIME THE PERSON WILL ACTUALLY SPEND IN PRISON.

↓ MAXIMUM SENTENCE ↓

SOME PEOPLE THINK ALL INMATES ARE RELEASED ONCE THEY HAVE SERVED THEIR MINIMUM SENTENCE. **THEY AREN'T**. INSTEAD, THE INMATE STARTS FROM THE MAXIMUM AND WORKS HIS WAY DOWN THROUGH EARNED TIME AND MERITORIOUS TIME.

MINIMUM SENTENCE

THE MINIMUM SENTENCE IS JUST THE LOWER LIMIT ON HOW MUCH THE SENTENCE MAY BE REDUCED. IN OTHER WORDS, NO MATTER HOW MUCH WORK HE DOES OR HOW MANY PROGRAMS HE COMPLETES, THE INMATE WILL NOT BE RELEASED BEFORE SERVING HIS MINIMUM SENTENCE.

MOST INMATES ARE NOT ABLE TO WORK THEIR SENTENCES ALL THE WAY DOWN TO THE MINIMUM. AVERAGE RELEASE DATES FOR EACH CLASS OF FELONY ARE SHOWN IN THE TABLE BELOW.

OFFENSE CLASS	PERCENT OF MINIMUM SERVED UPON RELEASE...
CLASS B1-C	102%
CLASS D	103%
CLASS E	104%
CLASS F	105%
CLASS G	107%
CLASS H	114%
CLASS I	113%

NOTICE THAT INMATES WITH MORE SERIOUS CONVICTIONS GENERALLY DO A BETTER JOB OF WORKING THEIR RELEASE DATES DOWN TOWARD THE MINIMUM SENTENCE. WHY? IT'S BECAUSE MANY INMATES WITH SHORTER SENTENCES AREN'T IN PRISON LONG ENOUGH TO COMPLETE PROGRAMS OR GET PLACED IN THE JOBS THAT EARN A LOT OF EARNED TIME.

LET'S PUT IT ALL TOGETHER FOR OUR EXAMPLE OF AN INMATE SERVING A 10-21 MONTH SENTENCE FOR A CLASS G FELONY. THE LAST 9 MONTHS OF HIS SENTENCE WILL BE SET ASIDE FOR PRS, LEAVING 10-12 MONTHS OF CONFINEMENT TO SERVE. ON AVERAGE, AN INMATE WITH A SENTENCE LIKE THAT WILL SERVE 107% OF HIS MINIMUM (10.7 MONTHS IN THIS CASE) BEFORE BEING RELEASED ONTO PRS. THE EARLIEST POSSIBLE RELEASE IS 10 MONTHS. THE LATEST IS 12 MONTHS.

10-12 MONTHS
CONFINEMENT PORTION

9 MONTHS
PRS PORTION

A FELONY INMATE'S SENTENCE IS NOT COMPLETE UPON RELEASE. ALL FELONS SERVE A TERM OF POST-RELEASE SUPERVISION (PRS) AFTER THEY ARE RELEASED FROM PRISON. IT'S MANDATORY—THE INMATE CANNOT REFUSE IT. THE LENGTH OF THE PRS TERM IS GOVERNED BY THE TYPE OF SENTENCE.

OFFENSE CLASS	LENGTH OF PRS
CLASS F–I	9 MONTHS
CLASS B1–E	12 MONTHS
SEX CRIME	60 MONTHS

DURING THE TERM OF PRS, THE PERSON IS SUPERVISED BY A PROBATION/PAROLE OFFICER—THE SAME OFFICERS WHO SUPERVISE PROBATIONERS IN NORTH CAROLINA.

WHAT ABOUT MULTIPLE SENTENCES?

MANY INMATES ARE SERVING TIME FOR MORE THAN ONE CONVICTION.

BY DEFAULT, SENTENCES RUN **CONCURRENTLY**. THAT MEANS THE INMATE SERVES THEM ALL AT ONCE AND GETS RELEASED WHEN THE LONGEST SENTENCE IS COMPLETE.

A JUDGE CAN ORDER **CONSECUTIVE SENTENCES**, SOMETIMES CALLED "BOXCAR" SENTENCES. THAT MEANS ONE SENTENCE DOES NOT BEGIN UNTIL THE ONE BEFORE IT ENDS. THE PRISON SYSTEM COMBINES CONSECUTIVE SENTENCES INTO A SINGLE SENTENCE WITH **ONE POST-RELEASE SUPERVISION PERIOD** AT THE END.

THEY WILL ADD UP ALL THE CONFINEMENT PORTIONS AND THEN ELIMINATE ALL OF THE PRS PORTIONS EXCEPT FOR THE LONGEST ONE. FOR EXAMPLE, IF AN INMATE HAD A 20–36 MONTH SENTENCE FOR A CLASS E FELONY FOLLOWED BY TWO 6–17 MONTH CLASS H FELONY SENTENCES, IT WOULD LOOK LIKE THIS:

ADD UP THE CONFINEMENT PORTIONS
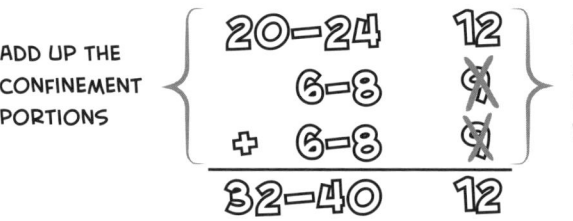
ELIMINATE ALL BUT THE LONGEST PRS PORTION

THE INMATE WILL SERVE BETWEEN 32 AND 40 MONTHS, DEPENDING ON EARNED TIME AND MERITORIOUS TIME, AND THEN BE RELEASED ONTO PRS FOR 12 MONTHS.

IF THE PERSON VIOLATES PRS, HE CAN BE BROUGHT BEFORE THE POST-RELEASE SUPERVISION AND PAROLE COMMISSION IN RALEIGH FOR A VIOLATION HEARING.

FOR SERIOUS VIOLATIONS (NEW CRIMES OR ABSCONDING), THE COMMISSION MAY REVOKE PRS AND ORDER THE PERSON BACK TO PRISON FOR THE TIME REMAINING ON HIS MAXIMUM SENTENCE (THE "EXTRA" 9, 12, OR 60 MONTHS THAT WERE AUTOMATICALLY SET ASIDE AS THE PRS PORTION AT THE BEGINNING OF THE SENTENCE). FOR OTHER VIOLATIONS (MISSED APPOINTMENTS, POSITIVE DRUG SCREENS, ETC.), HE COULD BE RETURNED TO PRISON FOR UP TO 3 MONTHS.

ONCE THE PRS PERIOD EXPIRES OR ALL THE TIME REMAINING ON THE REMAINING TERM OF IMPRISONMENT HAS BEEN SERVED, THE SENTENCE IS COMPLETE.

Jamie Markham is an associate professor of public law and government at the School of Government. He joined the faculty in 2007. His area of interest is criminal law and procedure, with a focus on the law of sentencing and corrections.

Shane Tharrington is the manager of classification and technical support for the prisons division of North Carolina's Department of Public Safety. He has worked in many capacities in the prison system for twenty-five years.

Jason Whitley is a painter, illustrator, and cartoonist. His portrait of Charlotte Hawkins Brown is in the Charlotte Hawkins Brown Museum. His newspaper comic strip, Sea Urchins, is collected into four books.

UNC
SCHOOL OF
GOVERNMENT

IN PRISON

9 781560 118992

ISBN-13: 978-1-56011-899-2

2017.04

This publication was printed and assembled by inmates and staff at the Correction Enterprises Print Plant.

CORRECTION
ENTERPRISES

Not Just Making It Right. Making It Better.

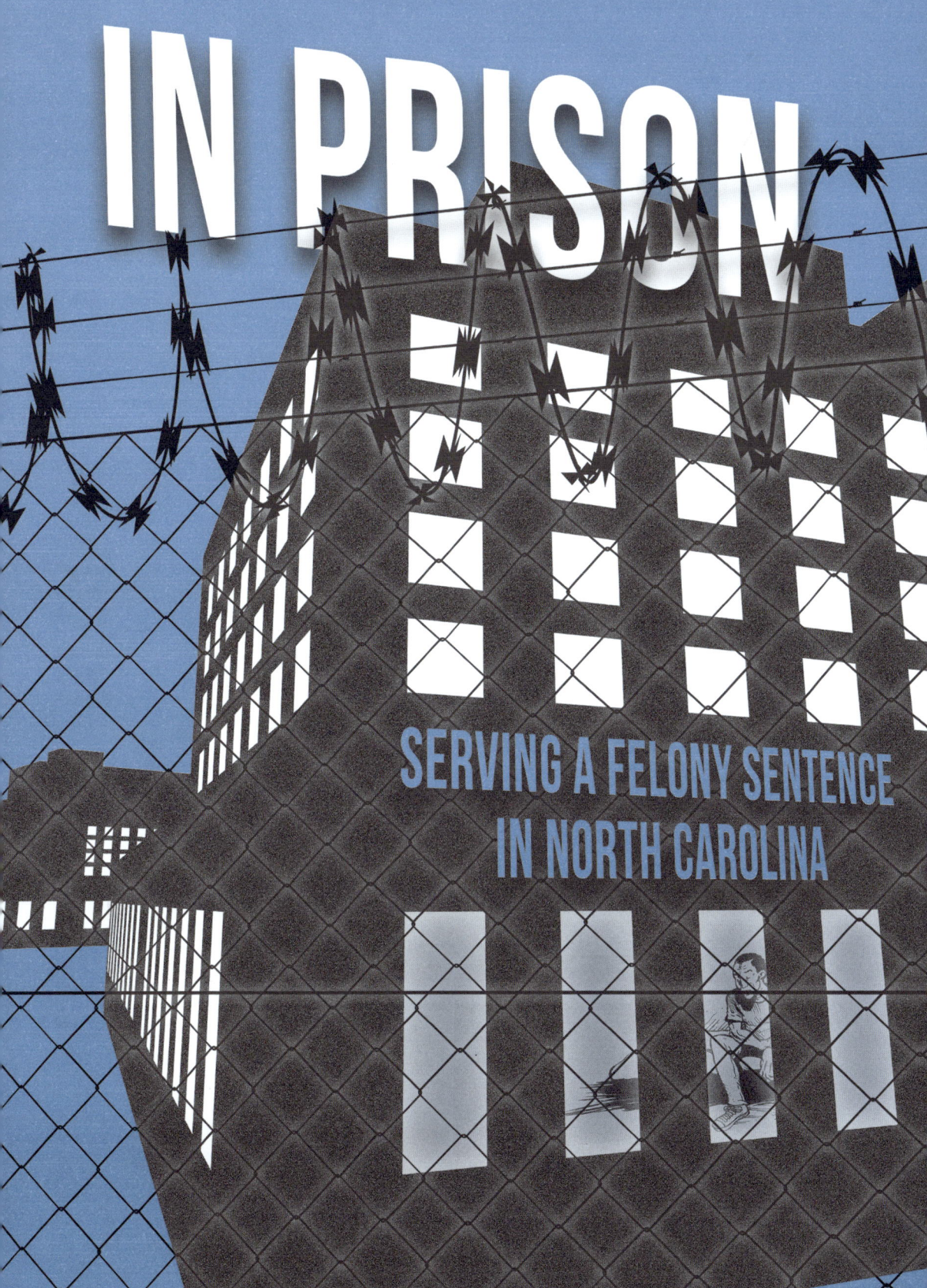

ISSUE NO. 1

JULY 2017

IN PRISON

SERVING A FELONY SENTENCE
IN NORTH CAROLINA

MARKHAM
THARRINGTON
WHITLEY

The School of Government at the University of North Carolina at Chapel Hill works to improve the lives of North Carolinians by engaging in practical scholarship that helps public officials and citizens understand and improve state and local government. Established in 1931 as the Institute of Government, the School provides educational, advisory, and research services for state and local governments. The School of Government is also home to a nationally ranked Master of Public Administration program, the North Carolina Judicial College, and specialized centers focused on community and economic development, information technology, and environmental finance.

As the largest university-based local government training, advisory, and research organization in the United States, the School of Government offers up to 200 courses, webinars, and specialized conferences for more than 12,000 public officials each year. In addition, faculty members annually publish approximately 50 books, manuals, reports, articles, bulletins, and other print and online content related to state and local government. The School also produces the *Daily Bulletin Online* each day the General Assembly is in session, reporting on activities for members of the legislature and others who need to follow the course of legislation.

Operating support for the School of Government's programs and activities comes from many sources, including state appropriations, local government membership dues, private contributions, publication sales, course fees, and service contracts.

Visit sog.unc.edu or call 919.966.5381 for more information on the School's courses, publications, programs, and services.

© 2017
School of Government
The University of North Carolina at Chapel Hill

Printed in the United States of America

21 20 19 18 17   1 2 3 4 5

ISBN 978-1-56011-899-2

∞ This publication is printed on permanent, acid-free paper in compliance with the North Carolina General Statutes.

♻ Printed on recycled paper

INTRODUCTION

This short book explains how a felony prison sentence is served in North Carolina. I hope those who read it will gain a better sense of where and how an inmate serves his or her time.

Presenting the information in illustrated form is by no means intended to make light of a very serious subject. It is, rather, offered as an accessible way to fill gaps in knowledge and to address common misperceptions about the way sentences are served. It is meant to give crime victims, defendants, inmates, and their families an understandable resource that translates the words and numbers on a sentencing judgment into a practical reality.

Though the book is of course not a comprehensive legal reference, I hope it will be useful to lawyers and judges, too. An improved understanding of how a sentence is administered should help you advise your clients, negotiate your pleas, and craft your judgments in a way that achieves a more refined measure of justice in each case.

I have neither the technical expertise nor the artistic talent to create something like this on my own. For the former, I relied on co-author Shane Tharrington, classification manager for North Carolina's Division of Adult Correction. For the latter, I turned to Jason Whitley, a talented illustrator who works as a creative lead for instructional innovation at the Eshelman School of Pharmacy at UNC-Chapel Hill. Many thanks to Shane (and to the prison system as a whole) for answering my many questions, and to Jason for turning my stick-figure storyboard into a real graphic novel.

Jamie Markham
Chapel Hill
September 2017

STORY BY
JAMIE MARKHAM AND
SHANE THARRINGTON

ART BY
JASON WHITLEY

THE DEFENDANT WILL BE HELD IN THE COUNTY JAIL UNTIL THE PRISON SYSTEM PICKS HIM UP, USUALLY WITHIN A WEEK OR SO.

IF THE DEFENDANT APPEALS HIS SENTENCE, HE COULD BE RELEASED ON AN APPEAL BOND, BUT THAT IS RARE.

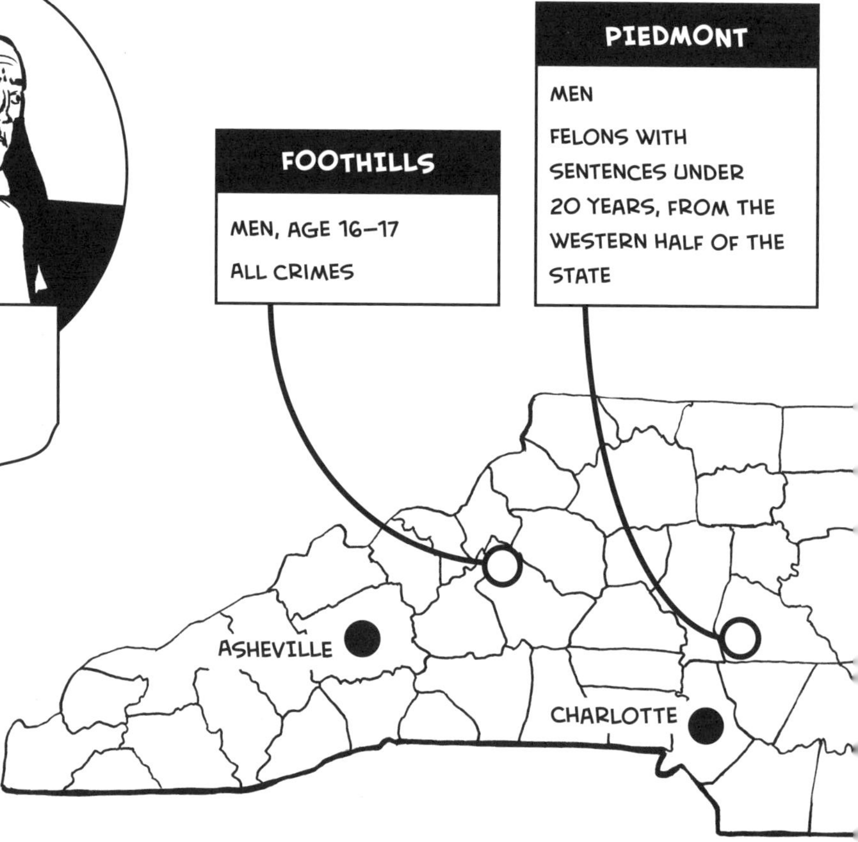

THE DEFENDANT'S FIRST STOP WILL BE ONE OF NORTH CAROLINA'S DIAGNOSTIC CENTERS.

FOOTHILLS

MEN, AGE 16–17

ALL CRIMES

PIEDMONT

MEN

FELONS WITH SENTENCES UNDER 20 YEARS, FROM THE WESTERN HALF OF THE STATE

ASHEVILLE

CHARLOTTE

NORTH CAROLINA'S DIAGNOSTIC CENTERS

THE DEFENDANT GENERALLY WILL GET JAIL CREDIT FOR ALL THE DAYS HE SPENT IN JAIL BEFORE CONVICTION.

JAIL CREDIT IS SUBTRACTED FROM BOTH THE MINIMUM AND MAXIMUM SENTENCE. FOR EXAMPLE, IF THE DEFENDANT HAD 2 MONTHS OF JAIL CREDIT, HE WOULD HAVE 8–19 MONTHS LEFT TO SERVE OF HIS 10–21 MONTH SENTENCE.

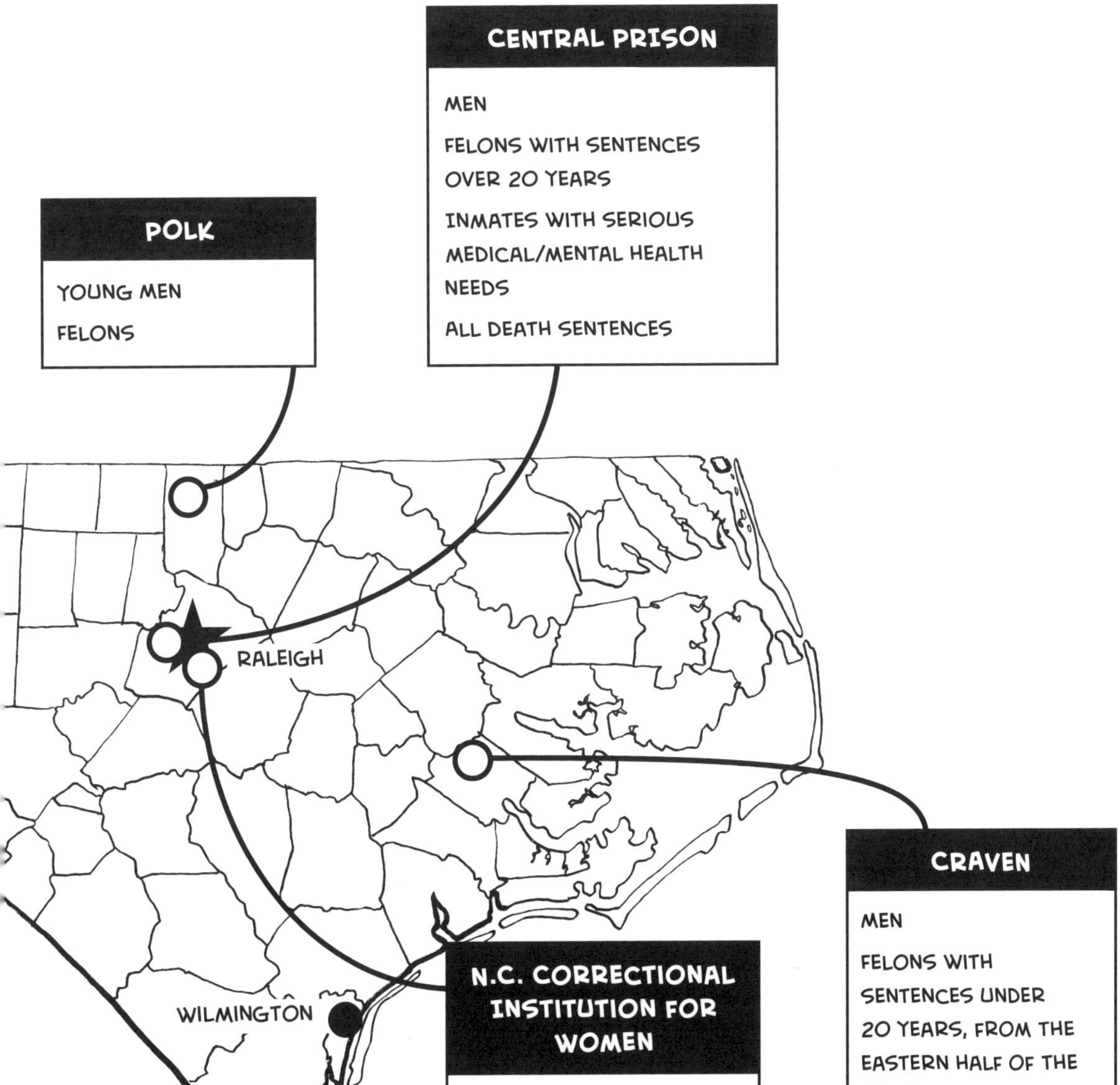

CENTRAL PRISON

MEN

FELONS WITH SENTENCES OVER 20 YEARS

INMATES WITH SERIOUS MEDICAL/MENTAL HEALTH NEEDS

ALL DEATH SENTENCES

POLK

YOUNG MEN

FELONS

RALEIGH

WILMINGTON

CRAVEN

MEN

FELONS WITH SENTENCES UNDER 20 YEARS, FROM THE EASTERN HALF OF THE STATE

N.C. CORRECTIONAL INSTITUTION FOR WOMEN

ALL WOMEN

THE DEFENDANT WILL SPEND 2-4 WEEKS AT THE DIAGNOSTIC FACILITY COMPLETING VARIOUS INPROCESSING ACTIVITES.

CLOTHING EXCHANGE

FINGERPRINTING

RISK-NEEDS ASSESSMENT

DNA SAMPLE

EYE EXAM

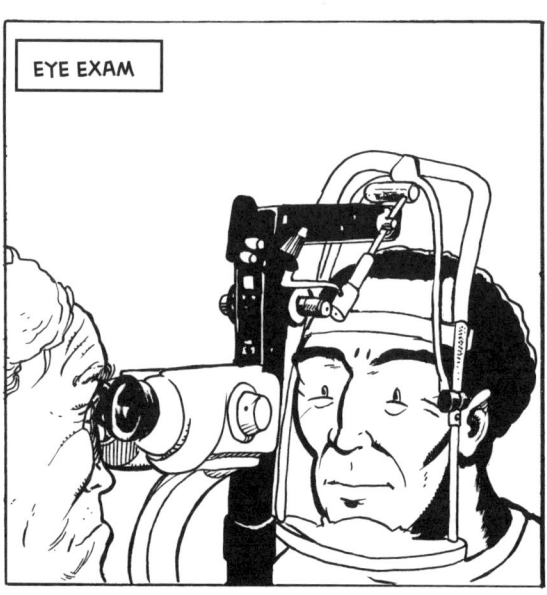

INTELLIGENCE TESTING

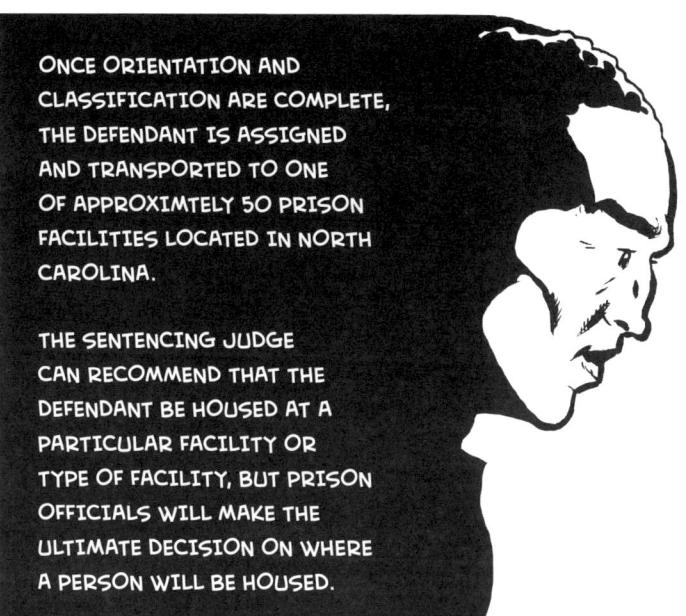

ONCE ORIENTATION AND CLASSIFICATION ARE COMPLETE, THE DEFENDANT IS ASSIGNED AND TRANSPORTED TO ONE OF APPROXIMTELY 50 PRISON FACILITIES LOCATED IN NORTH CAROLINA.

THE SENTENCING JUDGE CAN RECOMMEND THAT THE DEFENDANT BE HOUSED AT A PARTICULAR FACILITY OR TYPE OF FACILITY, BUT PRISON OFFICIALS WILL MAKE THE ULTIMATE DECISION ON WHERE A PERSON WILL BE HOUSED.

THE HOUSING DECISION IS BASED IN PART ON THE CUSTODY LEVEL TO WHICH THE INMATE IS ASSIGNED DURING CLASSIFICATION.

THERE ARE THREE MAIN CUSTODY LEVELS IN THE NORTH CAROLINA PRISON SYSTEM:

CLOSE CUSTODY (MOST SECURE)

MEDIUM CUSTODY

MINIMUM CUSTODY

THE MAP BELOW SHOWS SOME OF THE PRISONS TO WHICH AN INMATE MIGHT BE ASSIGNED. IT HIGHLIGHTS A SAMPLING OF THE SPECIAL PROGRAMS AND JOB ASSIGNMENTS AVAILABLE AT CERTAIN PRISONS. OVER THE COURSE OF SERVING A SENTENCE, SOME INMATES WILL TRANSFER BETWEEN FACILITIES AS CUSTODY LEVELS, WORK ASSIGNMENTS, AND PROGRAM NEEDS CHANGE.

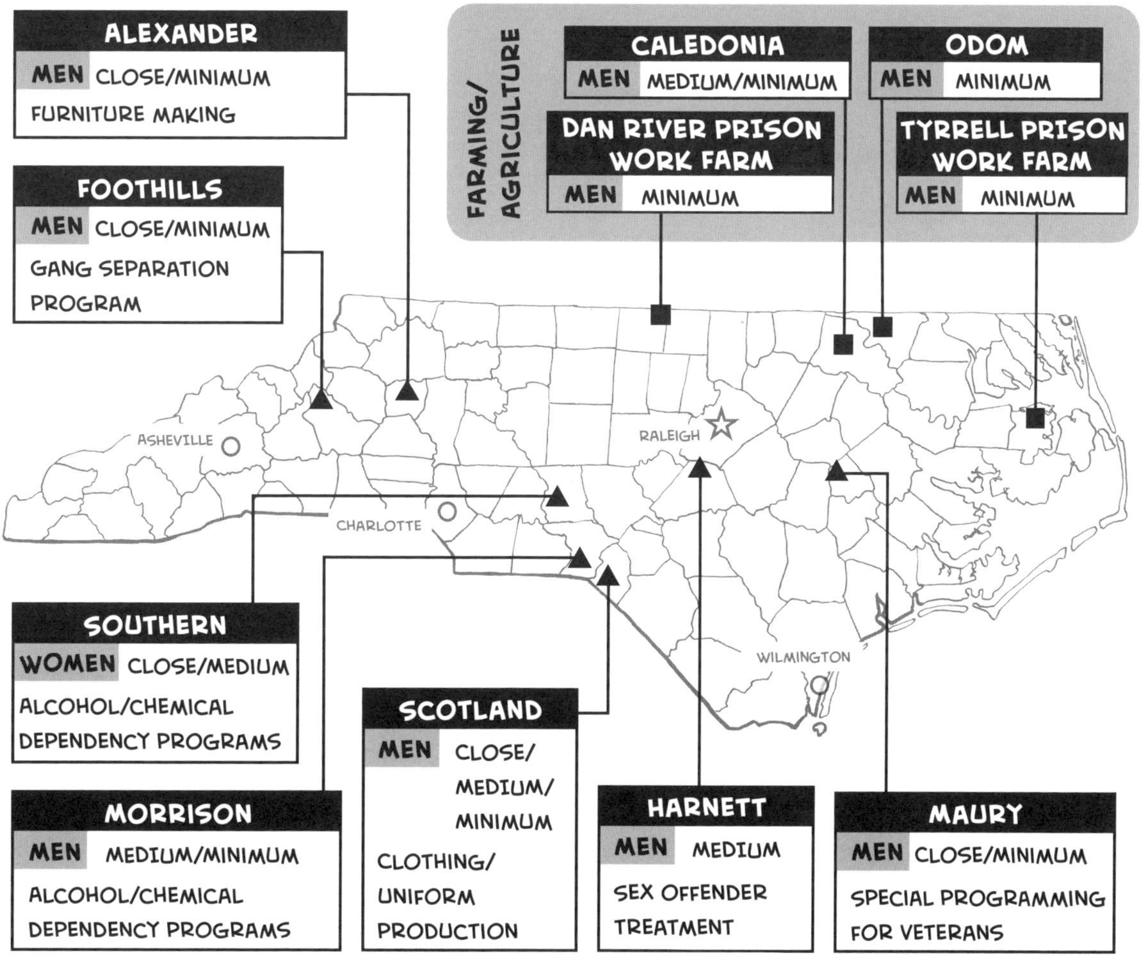

ALEXANDER
MEN CLOSE/MINIMUM
FURNITURE MAKING

FOOTHILLS
MEN CLOSE/MINIMUM
GANG SEPARATION PROGRAM

FARMING/AGRICULTURE

CALEDONIA
MEN MEDIUM/MINIMUM

DAN RIVER PRISON WORK FARM
MEN MINIMUM

ODOM
MEN MINIMUM

TYRRELL PRISON WORK FARM
MEN MINIMUM

ASHEVILLE

RALEIGH ☆

CHARLOTTE

SOUTHERN
WOMEN CLOSE/MEDIUM
ALCOHOL/CHEMICAL DEPENDENCY PROGRAMS

SCOTLAND
MEN CLOSE/MEDIUM/MINIMUM
CLOTHING/UNIFORM PRODUCTION

WILMINGTON

MORRISON
MEN MEDIUM/MINIMUM
ALCOHOL/CHEMICAL DEPENDENCY PROGRAMS

HARNETT
MEN MEDIUM
SEX OFFENDER TREATMENT

MAURY
MEN CLOSE/MINIMUM
SPECIAL PROGRAMMING FOR VETERANS

AT THE ASSIGNED FACLITY, THE INMATE BEGINS SERVING THE REMAINDER OF HIS SENTENCE. HOW LONG IT WILL TAKE TO SERVE IT DEPENDS IN PART ON WHAT HE DOES IN PRISON. PARTICIPATION IN WORK AND PROGRAMS ALLOWS AN INMATE TO EARN SENTENCE CREDITS CALLED **EARNED TIME**.

EARNED TIME IS AWARDED AT DIFFERENT RATES DEPENDING ON THE TYPE OF WORK OR PROGRAM COMPLETED. IN GENERAL, PARTICIPATION IN ANY OF THE JOBS OR PROGRAMS SHOWN BELOW WOULD BE REWARDED WITH 9 DAYS OF EARNED TIME PER MONTH.

EDUCATIONAL PROGRAMS

LAUNDRY

LICENSE PLATES

CONSTRUCTION

CUSTODIAL WORK

AN INMATE AWAITING A WORK OR PROGRAM ASSIGNMENT GENERALLY GETS 3 DAYS OF EARNED TIME PER MONTH.

INMATES CAN ALSO GET ANOTHER CREDIT CALLED **MERITORIOUS TIME** FOR EXEMPLARY ACTS, LIKE WORKING IN BAD WEATHER OR COMPLETING AN EDUCATIONAL DEGREE.

WELDING

ROAD SIGNS

TREATMENT GROUP

DOG TRAINING

ROAD WORK

KITCHEN WORK

SO WHEN IS AN INMATE RELEASED?

FELONY ACTIVE SENTENCES HAVE TWO PARTS: A PERIOD OF CONFINEMENT IN PRISON, FOLLOWED BY A PERIOD OF **POST-RELEASE SUPERVISION** (PRS). PRS IS A PERIOD OF SUPERVISED RELEASE IN THE COMMUNITY, SIMILAR TO PROBATION.

THE LENGTH OF THE PRS PORTION OF THE SENTENCE DEPENDS ON THE INMATE'S CLASS OF OFFENSE AND WHETHER OR NOT THE CRIME REQUIRES REGISTRATION AS A SEX OFFENDER.

OFFENSE CLASS	PRS PORTION OF MAXIMUM
CLASS F–I	9 MONTHS
CLASS B1–E	12 MONTHS
CLASS B1–E SEX CRIME	60 MONTHS

THE PRISON SYSTEM AUTOMATICALLY SUBTRACTS THE PRS PORTION OF THE SENTENCE FROM THE MAXIMUM AND SETS IT OFF TO THE SIDE. THAT'S BECAUSE THE INMATE WILL SERVE THAT TIME ONLY IF HIS POST-RELEASE SUPERVISION IS REVOKED. THE TIME THAT REMAINS AFTER SUBTRACTING THE PRS PORTION IS THE CONFINEMENT PORTION OF THE SENTENCE—THE TIME THE PERSON WILL ACTUALLY SPEND IN PRISON.

↓ MAXIMUM SENTENCE ↓

SOME PEOPLE THINK ALL INMATES ARE RELEASED ONCE THEY HAVE SERVED THEIR MINIMUM SENTENCE. **THEY AREN'T**. INSTEAD, THE INMATE STARTS FROM THE MAXIMUM AND WORKS HIS WAY DOWN THROUGH EARNED TIME AND MERITORIOUS TIME.

MINIMUM SENTENCE

THE MINIMUM SENTENCE IS JUST THE LOWER LIMIT ON HOW MUCH THE SENTENCE MAY BE REDUCED. IN OTHER WORDS, NO MATTER HOW MUCH WORK HE DOES OR HOW MANY PROGRAMS HE COMPLETES, THE INMATE WILL NOT BE RELEASED BEFORE SERVING HIS MINIMUM SENTENCE.

MOST INMATES ARE NOT ABLE TO WORK THEIR SENTENCES ALL THE WAY DOWN TO THE MINIMUM. AVERAGE RELEASE DATES FOR EACH CLASS OF FELONY ARE SHOWN IN THE TABLE BELOW.

OFFENSE CLASS	PERCENT OF MINIMUM SERVED UPON RELEASE...
CLASS B1–C	102%
CLASS D	103%
CLASS E	104%
CLASS F	105%
CLASS G	107%
CLASS H	114%
CLASS I	113%

NOTICE THAT INMATES WITH MORE SERIOUS CONVICTIONS GENERALLY DO A BETTER JOB OF WORKING THEIR RELEASE DATES DOWN TOWARD THE MINIMUM SENTENCE. WHY? IT'S BECAUSE MANY INMATES WITH SHORTER SENTENCES AREN'T IN PRISON LONG ENOUGH TO COMPLETE PROGRAMS OR GET PLACED IN THE JOBS THAT EARN A LOT OF EARNED TIME.

LET'S PUT IT ALL TOGETHER FOR OUR EXAMPLE OF AN INMATE SERVING A 10–21 MONTH SENTENCE FOR A CLASS G FELONY. THE LAST 9 MONTHS OF HIS SENTENCE WILL BE SET ASIDE FOR PRS, LEAVING 10–12 MONTHS OF CONFINEMENT TO SERVE. ON AVERAGE, AN INMATE WITH A SENTENCE LIKE THAT WILL SERVE 107% OF HIS MINIMUM (10.7 MONTHS IN THIS CASE) BEFORE BEING RELEASED ONTO PRS. THE EARLIEST POSSIBLE RELEASE IS 10 MONTHS. THE LATEST IS 12 MONTHS.

CONFINEMENT PORTION  PRS PORTION

A FELONY INMATE'S SENTENCE IS NOT COMPLETE UPON RELEASE. ALL FELONS SERVE A TERM OF POST-RELEASE SUPERVISION (PRS) AFTER THEY ARE RELEASED FROM PRISON. IT'S MANDATORY—THE INMATE CANNOT REFUSE IT. THE LENGTH OF THE PRS TERM IS GOVERNED BY THE TYPE OF SENTENCE.

OFFENSE CLASS	LENGTH OF PRS
CLASS F–I	9 MONTHS
CLASS B1–E	12 MONTHS
SEX CRIME	60 MONTHS

DURING THE TERM OF PRS, THE PERSON IS SUPERVISED BY A PROBATION/PAROLE OFFICER—THE SAME OFFICERS WHO SUPERVISE PROBATIONERS IN NORTH CAROLINA.

WHAT ABOUT MULTIPLE SENTENCES?

MANY INMATES ARE SERVING TIME FOR MORE THAN ONE CONVICTION.

BY DEFAULT, SENTENCES RUN **CONCURRENTLY**. THAT MEANS THE INMATE SERVES THEM ALL AT ONCE AND GETS RELEASED WHEN THE LONGEST SENTENCE IS COMPLETE.

A JUDGE CAN ORDER **CONSECUTIVE SENTENCES**, SOMETIMES CALLED "BOXCAR" SENTENCES. THAT MEANS ONE SENTENCE DOES NOT BEGIN UNTIL THE ONE BEFORE IT ENDS. THE PRISON SYSTEM COMBINES CONSECUTIVE SENTENCES INTO A SINGLE SENTENCE WITH **ONE POST-RELEASE SUPERVISION PERIOD** AT THE END.

THEY WILL ADD UP ALL THE CONFINEMENT PORTIONS AND THEN ELIMINATE ALL OF THE PRS PORTIONS EXCEPT FOR THE LONGEST ONE. FOR EXAMPLE, IF AN INMATE HAD A 20–36 MONTH SENTENCE FOR A CLASS E FELONY FOLLOWED BY TWO 6–17 MONTH CLASS H FELONY SENTENCES, IT WOULD LOOK LIKE THIS:

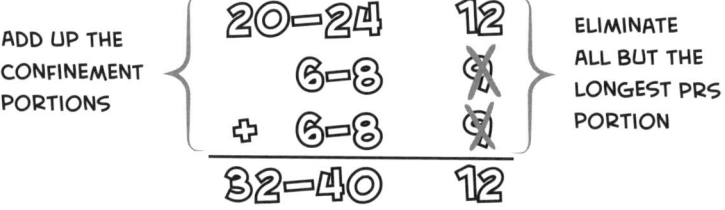

ADD UP THE CONFINEMENT PORTIONS

ELIMINATE ALL BUT THE LONGEST PRS PORTION

THE INMATE WILL SERVE BETWEEN 32 AND 40 MONTHS, DEPENDING ON EARNED TIME AND MERITORIOUS TIME, AND THEN BE RELEASED ONTO PRS FOR 12 MONTHS.

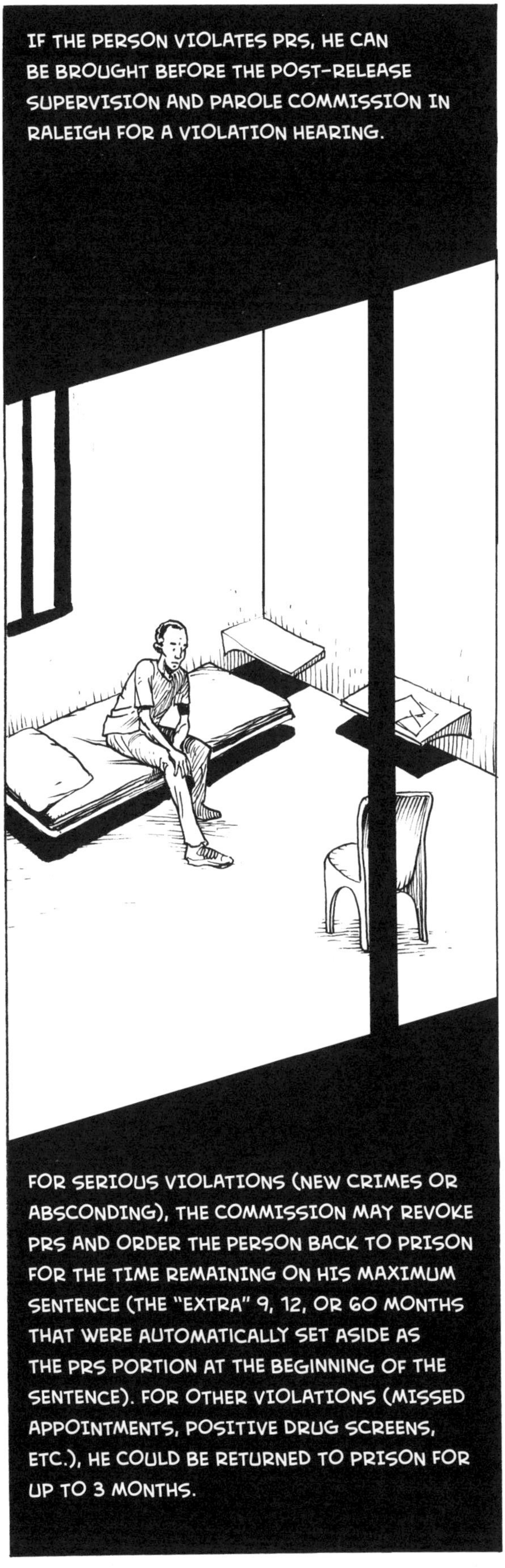

IF THE PERSON VIOLATES PRS, HE CAN BE BROUGHT BEFORE THE POST-RELEASE SUPERVISION AND PAROLE COMMISSION IN RALEIGH FOR A VIOLATION HEARING.

FOR SERIOUS VIOLATIONS (NEW CRIMES OR ABSCONDING), THE COMMISSION MAY REVOKE PRS AND ORDER THE PERSON BACK TO PRISON FOR THE TIME REMAINING ON HIS MAXIMUM SENTENCE (THE "EXTRA" 9, 12, OR 60 MONTHS THAT WERE AUTOMATICALLY SET ASIDE AS THE PRS PORTION AT THE BEGINNING OF THE SENTENCE). FOR OTHER VIOLATIONS (MISSED APPOINTMENTS, POSITIVE DRUG SCREENS, ETC.), HE COULD BE RETURNED TO PRISON FOR UP TO 3 MONTHS.

ONCE THE PRS PERIOD EXPIRES OR ALL THE TIME REMAINING ON THE REMAINING TERM OF IMPRISONMENT HAS BEEN SERVED, THE SENTENCE IS COMPLETE.

Jamie Markham is an associate professor of public law and government at the School of Government. He joined the faculty in 2007. His area of interest is criminal law and procedure, with a focus on the law of sentencing and corrections.

Shane Tharrington is the manager of classification and technical support for the prisons division of North Carolina's Department of Public Safety. He has worked in many capacities in the prison system for twenty-five years.

Jason Whitley is a painter, illustrator, and cartoonist. His portrait of Charlotte Hawkins Brown is in the Charlotte Hawkins Brown Museum. His newspaper comic strip, Sea Urchins, is collected into four books.

UNC
SCHOOL OF
GOVERNMENT

This publication was printed and assembled by inmates and staff at the Correction Enterprises Print Plant.

CORRECTION
ENTERPRISES

Not Just Making It Right. Making It Better.

ISBN-13: 978-1-56011-899-2

2017.04

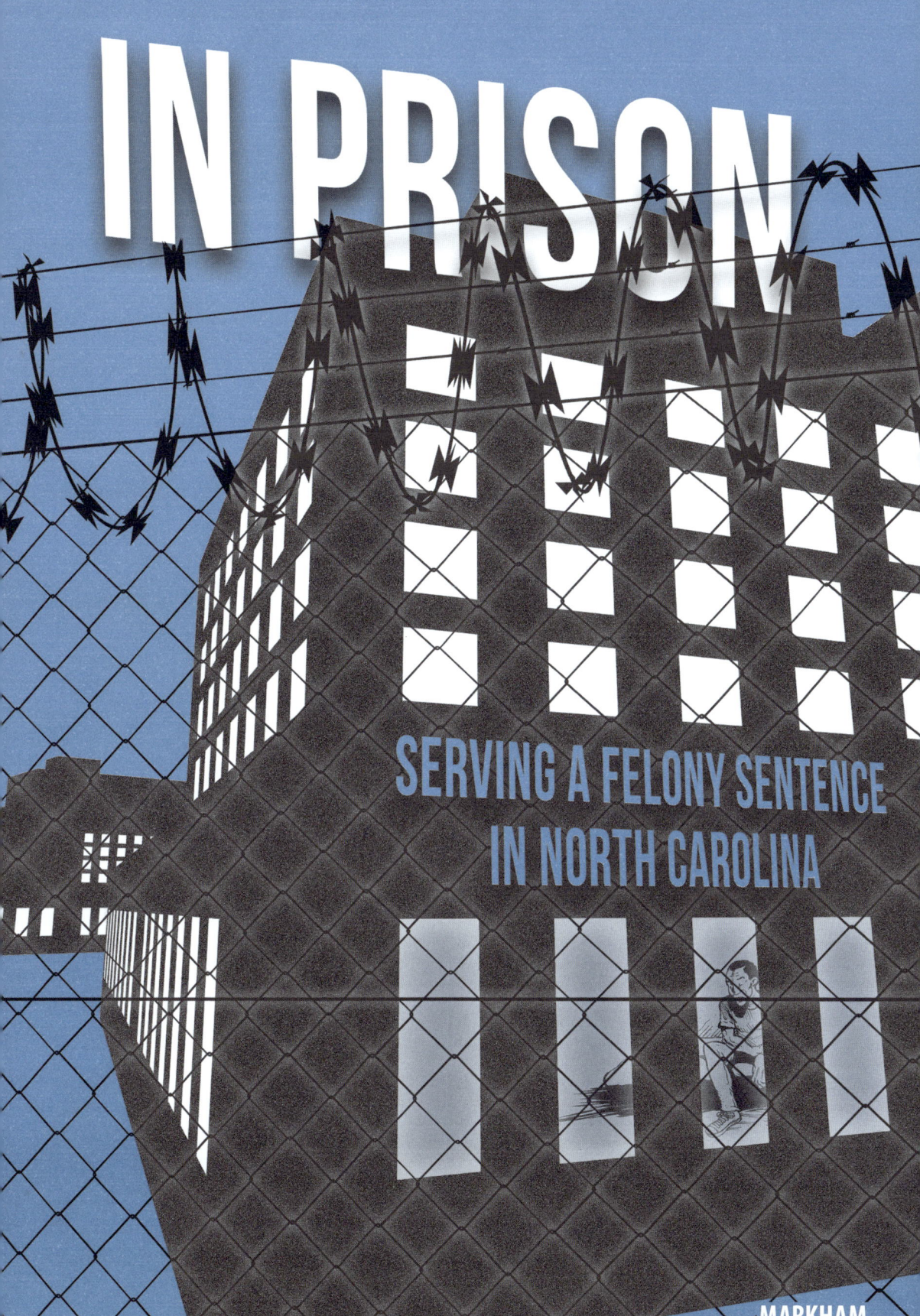

IN PRISON

SERVING A FELONY SENTENCE IN NORTH CAROLINA

MARKHAM
THARRINGTON
WHITLEY

The School of Government at the University of North Carolina at Chapel Hill works to improve the lives of North Carolinians by engaging in practical scholarship that helps public officials and citizens understand and improve state and local government. Established in 1931 as the Institute of Government, the School provides educational, advisory, and research services for state and local governments. The School of Government is also home to a nationally ranked Master of Public Administration program, the North Carolina Judicial College, and specialized centers focused on community and economic development, information technology, and environmental finance.

As the largest university-based local government training, advisory, and research organization in the United States, the School of Government offers up to 200 courses, webinars, and specialized conferences for more than 12,000 public officials each year. In addition, faculty members annually publish approximately 50 books, manuals, reports, articles, bulletins, and other print and online content related to state and local government. The School also produces the *Daily Bulletin Online* each day the General Assembly is in session, reporting on activities for members of the legislature and others who need to follow the course of legislation.

Operating support for the School of Government's programs and activities comes from many sources, including state appropriations, local government membership dues, private contributions, publication sales, course fees, and service contracts.

Visit sog.unc.edu or call 919.966.5381 for more information on the School's courses, publications, programs, and services.

© 2017
School of Government
The University of North Carolina at Chapel Hill

Printed in the United States of America

21 20 19 18 17   1 2 3 4 5

ISBN 978-1-56011-899-2

∞ This publication is printed on permanent, acid-free paper in compliance with the North Carolina General Statutes.

♲ Printed on recycled paper

INTRODUCTION

T his short book explains how a felony prison sentence is served in North Carolina. I hope those who read it will gain a better sense of where and how an inmate serves his or her time.

Presenting the information in illustrated form is by no means intended to make light of a very serious subject. It is, rather, offered as an accessible way to fill gaps in knowledge and to address common misperceptions about the way sentences are served. It is meant to give crime victims, defendants, inmates, and their families an understandable resource that translates the words and numbers on a sentencing judgment into a practical reality.

Though the book is of course not a comprehensive legal reference, I hope it will be useful to lawyers and judges, too. An improved understanding of how a sentence is administered should help you advise your clients, negotiate your pleas, and craft your judgments in a way that achieves a more refined measure of justice in each case.

I have neither the technical expertise nor the artistic talent to create something like this on my own. For the former, I relied on co-author Shane Tharrington, classification manager for North Carolina's Division of Adult Correction. For the latter, I turned to Jason Whitley, a talented illustrator who works as a creative lead for instructional innovation at the Eshelman School of Pharmacy at UNC-Chapel Hill. Many thanks to Shane (and to the prison system as a whole) for answering my many questions, and to Jason for turning my stick-figure storyboard into a real graphic novel.

Jamie Markham
Chapel Hill
September 2017

THE DEFENDANT WILL BE HELD IN THE COUNTY JAIL UNTIL THE PRISON SYSTEM PICKS HIM UP, USUALLY WITHIN A WEEK OR SO.

IF THE DEFENDANT APPEALS HIS SENTENCE, HE COULD BE RELEASED ON AN APPEAL BOND, BUT THAT IS RARE.

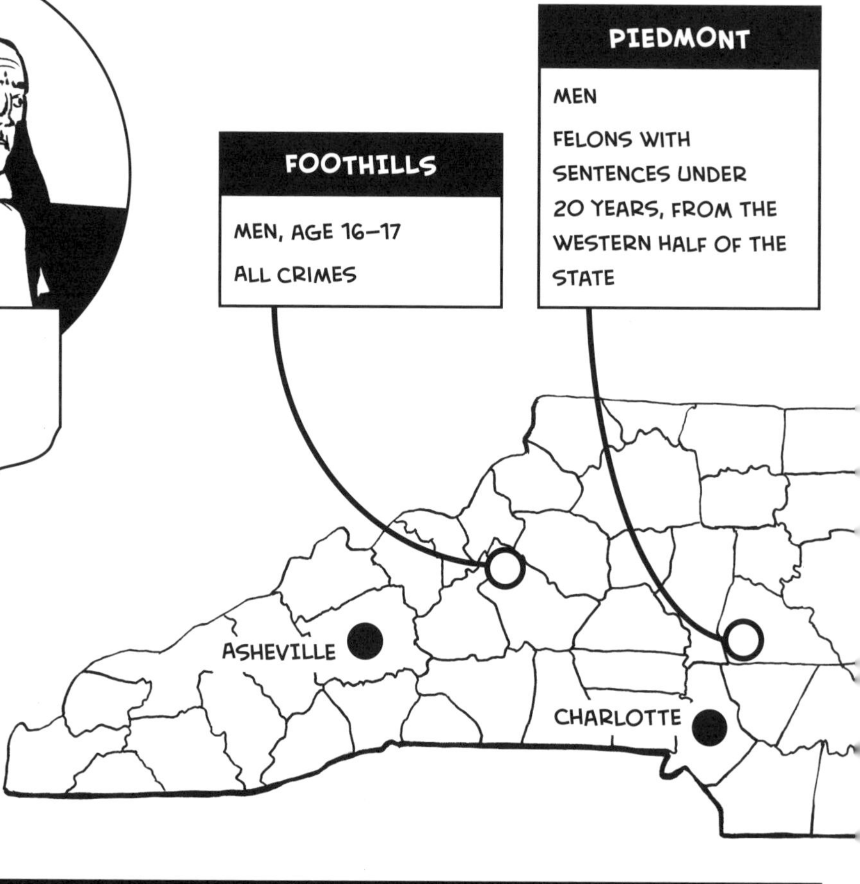

THE DEFENDANT'S FIRST STOP WILL BE ONE OF NORTH CAROLINA'S DIAGNOSTIC CENTERS.

FOOTHILLS

MEN, AGE 16-17

ALL CRIMES

PIEDMONT

MEN

FELONS WITH SENTENCES UNDER 20 YEARS, FROM THE WESTERN HALF OF THE STATE

ASHEVILLE

CHARLOTTE

NORTH CAROLINA'S DIAGNOSTIC CENTERS

THE DEFENDANT GENERALLY WILL GET JAIL CREDIT FOR ALL THE DAYS HE SPENT IN JAIL BEFORE CONVICTION.

JAIL CREDIT IS SUBTRACTED FROM BOTH THE MINIMUM AND MAXIMUM SENTENCE. FOR EXAMPLE, IF THE DEFENDANT HAD 2 MONTHS OF JAIL CREDIT, HE WOULD HAVE 8–19 MONTHS LEFT TO SERVE OF HIS 10–21 MONTH SENTENCE.

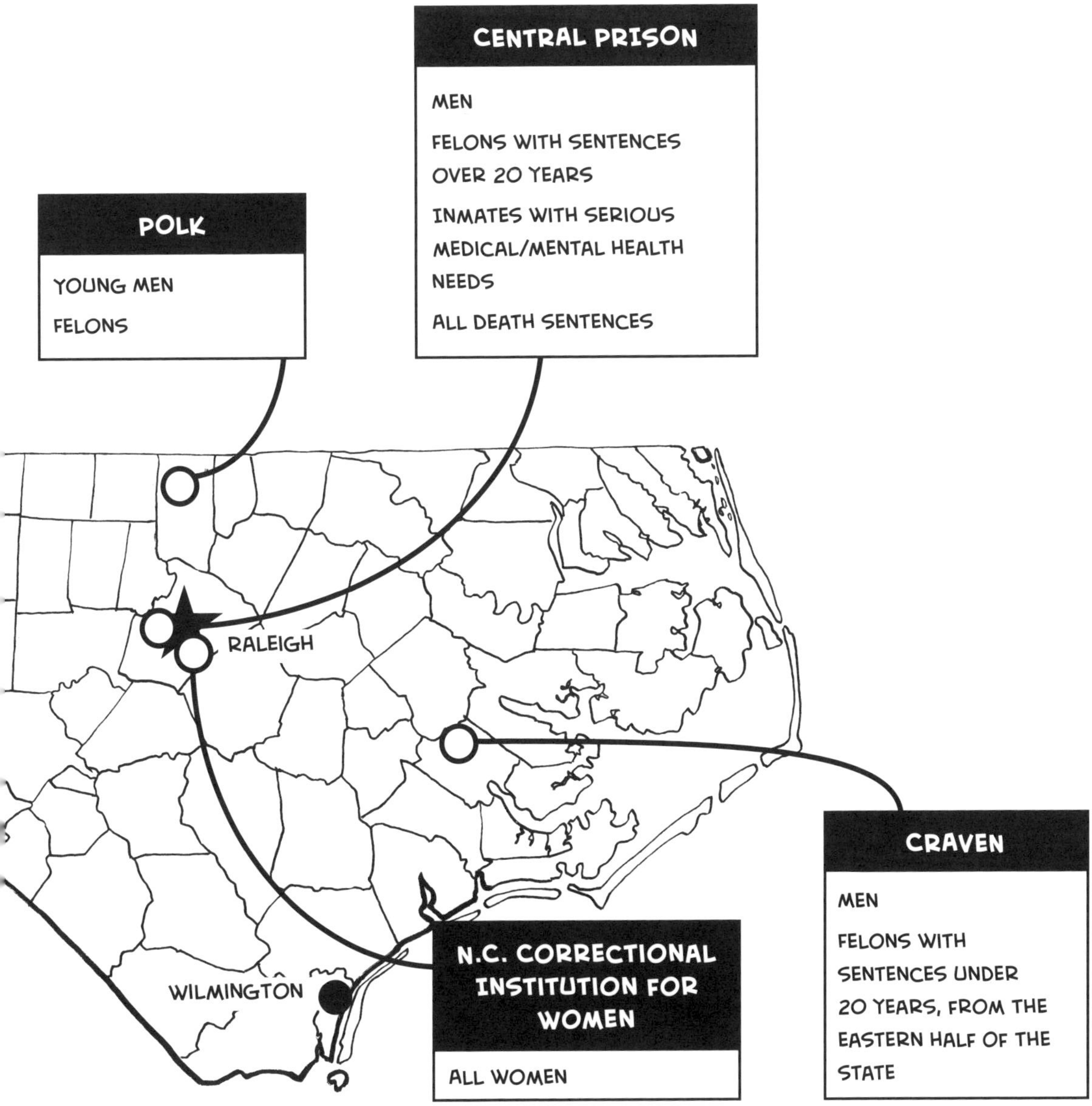

CENTRAL PRISON

MEN

FELONS WITH SENTENCES OVER 20 YEARS

INMATES WITH SERIOUS MEDICAL/MENTAL HEALTH NEEDS

ALL DEATH SENTENCES

POLK

YOUNG MEN

FELONS

RALEIGH

CRAVEN

MEN

FELONS WITH SENTENCES UNDER 20 YEARS, FROM THE EASTERN HALF OF THE STATE

WILMINGTON

N.C. CORRECTIONAL INSTITUTION FOR WOMEN

ALL WOMEN

THE DEFENDANT WILL SPEND 2–4 WEEKS AT THE DIAGNOSTIC FACILITY COMPLETING VARIOUS INPROCESSING ACTIVITES.

CLOTHING EXCHANGE

FINGERPRINTING

RISK-NEEDS ASSESSMENT

DNA SAMPLE

EYE EXAM

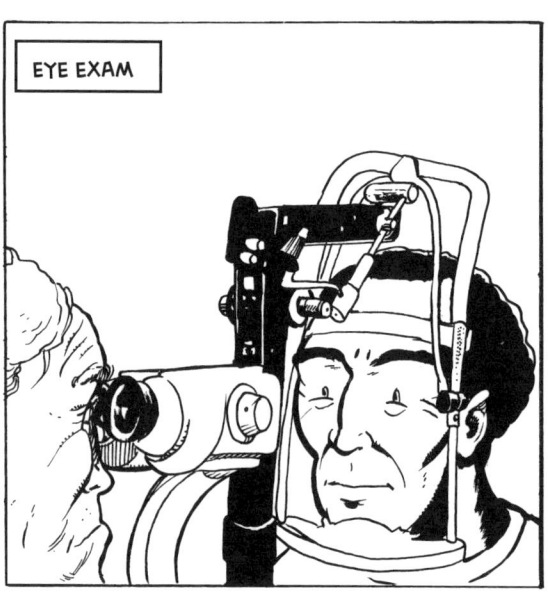

INTELLIGENCE TESTING

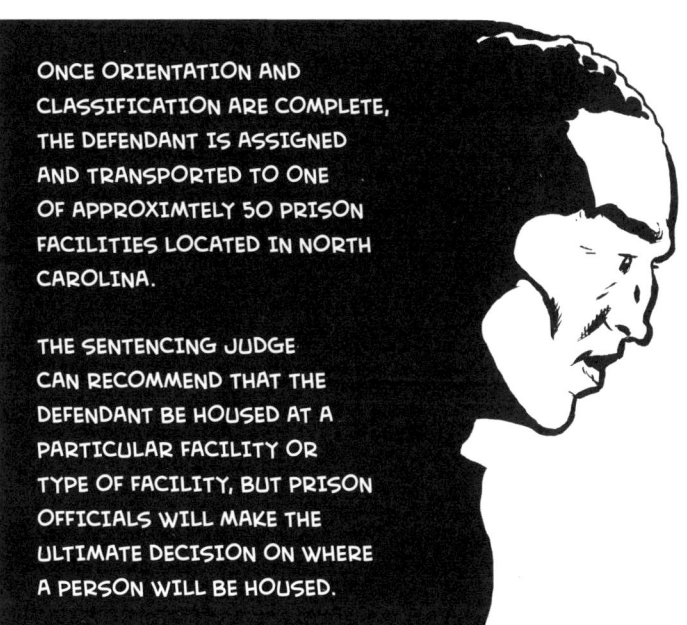

ONCE ORIENTATION AND CLASSIFICATION ARE COMPLETE, THE DEFENDANT IS ASSIGNED AND TRANSPORTED TO ONE OF APPROXIMTELY 50 PRISON FACILITIES LOCATED IN NORTH CAROLINA.

THE SENTENCING JUDGE CAN RECOMMEND THAT THE DEFENDANT BE HOUSED AT A PARTICULAR FACILITY OR TYPE OF FACILITY, BUT PRISON OFFICIALS WILL MAKE THE ULTIMATE DECISION ON WHERE A PERSON WILL BE HOUSED.

THE HOUSING DECISION IS BASED IN PART ON THE CUSTODY LEVEL TO WHICH THE INMATE IS ASSIGNED DURING CLASSIFICATION.

THERE ARE THREE MAIN CUSTODY LEVELS IN THE NORTH CAROLINA PRISON SYSTEM:

CLOSE CUSTODY (MOST SECURE)

MEDIUM CUSTODY

MINIMUM CUSTODY

THE MAP BELOW SHOWS SOME OF THE PRISONS TO WHICH AN INMATE MIGHT BE ASSIGNED. IT HIGHLIGHTS A SAMPLING OF THE SPECIAL PROGRAMS AND JOB ASSIGNMENTS AVAILABLE AT CERTAIN PRISONS. OVER THE COURSE OF SERVING A SENTENCE, SOME INMATES WILL TRANSFER BETWEEN FACILITIES AS CUSTODY LEVELS, WORK ASSIGNMENTS, AND PROGRAM NEEDS CHANGE.

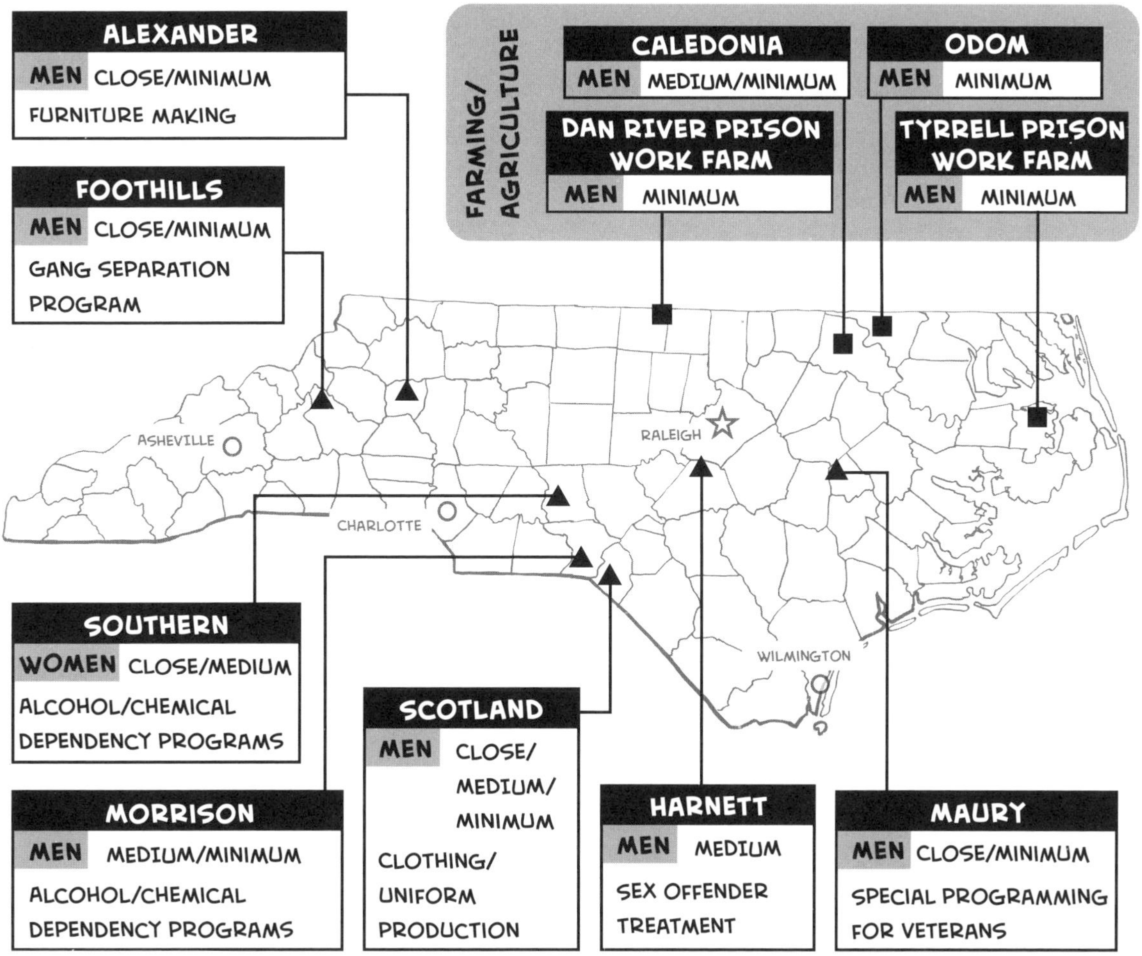

ALEXANDER
MEN CLOSE/MINIMUM
FURNITURE MAKING

FOOTHILLS
MEN CLOSE/MINIMUM
GANG SEPARATION PROGRAM

FARMING/AGRICULTURE

CALEDONIA
MEN MEDIUM/MINIMUM

ODOM
MEN MINIMUM

DAN RIVER PRISON WORK FARM
MEN MINIMUM

TYRRELL PRISON WORK FARM
MEN MINIMUM

ASHEVILLE
RALEIGH
CHARLOTTE
WILMINGTON

SOUTHERN
WOMEN CLOSE/MEDIUM
ALCOHOL/CHEMICAL DEPENDENCY PROGRAMS

SCOTLAND
MEN CLOSE/ MEDIUM/ MINIMUM
CLOTHING/ UNIFORM PRODUCTION

MORRISON
MEN MEDIUM/MINIMUM
ALCOHOL/CHEMICAL DEPENDENCY PROGRAMS

HARNETT
MEN MEDIUM
SEX OFFENDER TREATMENT

MAURY
MEN CLOSE/MINIMUM
SPECIAL PROGRAMMING FOR VETERANS

AT THE ASSIGNED FACILITY, THE INMATE BEGINS SERVING THE REMAINDER OF HIS SENTENCE. HOW LONG IT WILL TAKE TO SERVE IT DEPENDS IN PART ON WHAT HE DOES IN PRISON. PARTICIPATION IN WORK AND PROGRAMS ALLOWS AN INMATE TO EARN SENTENCE CREDITS CALLED **EARNED TIME.**

EARNED TIME IS AWARDED AT DIFFERENT RATES DEPENDING ON THE TYPE OF WORK OR PROGRAM COMPLETED. IN GENERAL, PARTICIPATION IN ANY OF THE JOBS OR PROGRAMS SHOWN BELOW WOULD BE REWARDED WITH 9 DAYS OF EARNED TIME PER MONTH.

EDUCATIONAL PROGRAMS

LAUNDRY

LICENSE PLATES

CONSTRUCTION

CUSTODIAL WORK

AN INMATE AWAITING A WORK OR PROGRAM ASSIGNMENT GENERALLY GETS 3 DAYS OF EARNED TIME PER MONTH.

INMATES CAN ALSO GET ANOTHER CREDIT CALLED **MERITORIOUS TIME** FOR EXEMPLARY ACTS, LIKE WORKING IN BAD WEATHER OR COMPLETING AN EDUCATIONAL DEGREE.

WELDING

ROAD SIGNS

TREATMENT GROUP

DOG TRAINING

ROAD WORK

KITCHEN WORK

SO WHEN IS AN INMATE RELEASED?

FELONY ACTIVE SENTENCES HAVE TWO PARTS: A PERIOD OF CONFINEMENT IN PRISON, FOLLOWED BY A PERIOD OF **POST-RELEASE SUPERVISION** (PRS). PRS IS A PERIOD OF SUPERVISED RELEASE IN THE COMMUNITY, SIMILAR TO PROBATION.

THE LENGTH OF THE PRS PORTION OF THE SENTENCE DEPENDS ON THE INMATE'S CLASS OF OFFENSE AND WHETHER OR NOT THE CRIME REQUIRES REGISTRATION AS A SEX OFFENDER.

OFFENSE CLASS	PRS PORTION OF MAXIMUM
CLASS F-I	9 MONTHS
CLASS B1-E	12 MONTHS
CLASS B1-E SEX CRIME	60 MONTHS

THE PRISON SYSTEM AUTOMATICALLY SUBTRACTS THE PRS PORTION OF THE SENTENCE FROM THE MAXIMUM AND SETS IT OFF TO THE SIDE. THAT'S BECAUSE THE INMATE WILL SERVE THAT TIME ONLY IF HIS POST-RELEASE SUPERVISION IS REVOKED. THE TIME THAT REMAINS AFTER SUBTRACTING THE PRS PORTION IS THE CONFINEMENT PORTION OF THE SENTENCE—THE TIME THE PERSON WILL ACTUALLY SPEND IN PRISON.

↓ MAXIMUM SENTENCE ↓

SOME PEOPLE THINK ALL INMATES ARE RELEASED ONCE THEY HAVE SERVED THEIR MINIMUM SENTENCE. **THEY AREN'T**. INSTEAD, THE INMATE STARTS FROM THE MAXIMUM AND WORKS HIS WAY DOWN THROUGH EARNED TIME AND MERITORIOUS TIME.

EXIT

MINIMUM SENTENCE

THE MINIMUM SENTENCE IS JUST THE LOWER LIMIT ON HOW MUCH THE SENTENCE MAY BE REDUCED. IN OTHER WORDS, NO MATTER HOW MUCH WORK HE DOES OR HOW MANY PROGRAMS HE COMPLETES, THE INMATE WILL NOT BE RELEASED BEFORE SERVING HIS MINIMUM SENTENCE.

MOST INMATES ARE NOT ABLE TO WORK THEIR SENTENCES ALL THE WAY DOWN TO THE MINIMUM. AVERAGE RELEASE DATES FOR EACH CLASS OF FELONY ARE SHOWN IN THE TABLE BELOW.

OFFENSE CLASS	PERCENT OF MINIMUM SERVED UPON RELEASE...
CLASS B1–C	102%
CLASS D	103%
CLASS E	104%
CLASS F	105%
CLASS G	107%
CLASS H	114%
CLASS I	113%

NOTICE THAT INMATES WITH MORE SERIOUS CONVICTIONS GENERALLY DO A BETTER JOB OF WORKING THEIR RELEASE DATES DOWN TOWARD THE MINIMUM SENTENCE. WHY? IT'S BECAUSE MANY INMATES WITH SHORTER SENTENCES AREN'T IN PRISON LONG ENOUGH TO COMPLETE PROGRAMS OR GET PLACED IN THE JOBS THAT EARN A LOT OF EARNED TIME.

LET'S PUT IT ALL TOGETHER FOR OUR EXAMPLE OF AN INMATE SERVING A 10–21 MONTH SENTENCE FOR A CLASS G FELONY. THE LAST 9 MONTHS OF HIS SENTENCE WILL BE SET ASIDE FOR PRS, LEAVING 10–12 MONTHS OF CONFINEMENT TO SERVE. ON AVERAGE, AN INMATE WITH A SENTENCE LIKE THAT WILL SERVE 107% OF HIS MINIMUM (10.7 MONTHS IN THIS CASE) BEFORE BEING RELEASED ONTO PRS. THE EARLIEST POSSIBLE RELEASE IS 10 MONTHS. THE LATEST IS 12 MONTHS.

10–12 MONTHS

CONFINEMENT PORTION

9 MONTHS

PRS PORTION

A FELONY INMATE'S SENTENCE IS NOT COMPLETE UPON RELEASE. ALL FELONS SERVE A TERM OF POST-RELEASE SUPERVISION (PRS) AFTER THEY ARE RELEASED FROM PRISON. IT'S MANDATORY—THE INMATE CANNOT REFUSE IT. THE LENGTH OF THE PRS TERM IS GOVERNED BY THE TYPE OF SENTENCE.

OFFENSE CLASS	LENGTH OF PRS
CLASS F–I	9 MONTHS
CLASS B1–E	12 MONTHS
SEX CRIME	60 MONTHS

DURING THE TERM OF PRS, THE PERSON IS SUPERVISED BY A PROBATION/PAROLE OFFICER—THE SAME OFFICERS WHO SUPERVISE PROBATIONERS IN NORTH CAROLINA.

WHAT ABOUT MULTIPLE SENTENCES?

MANY INMATES ARE SERVING TIME FOR MORE THAN ONE CONVICTION.

BY DEFAULT, SENTENCES RUN **CONCURRENTLY.** THAT MEANS THE INMATE SERVES THEM ALL AT ONCE AND GETS RELEASED WHEN THE LONGEST SENTENCE IS COMPLETE.

A JUDGE CAN ORDER **CONSECUTIVE SENTENCES,** SOMETIMES CALLED "BOXCAR" SENTENCES. THAT MEANS ONE SENTENCE DOES NOT BEGIN UNTIL THE ONE BEFORE IT ENDS. THE PRISON SYSTEM COMBINES CONSECUTIVE SENTENCES INTO A SINGLE SENTENCE WITH **ONE POST-RELEASE SUPERVISION PERIOD** AT THE END.

THEY WILL ADD UP ALL THE CONFINEMENT PORTIONS AND THEN ELIMINATE ALL OF THE PRS PORTIONS EXCEPT FOR THE LONGEST ONE. FOR EXAMPLE, IF AN INMATE HAD A 20–36 MONTH SENTENCE FOR A CLASS E FELONY FOLLOWED BY TWO 6–17 MONTH CLASS H FELONY SENTENCES, IT WOULD LOOK LIKE THIS:

ADD UP THE CONFINEMENT PORTIONS

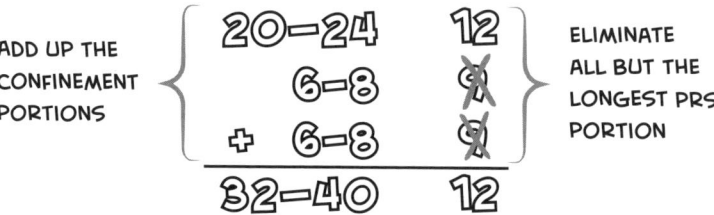

ELIMINATE ALL BUT THE LONGEST PRS PORTION

THE INMATE WILL SERVE BETWEEN 32 AND 40 MONTHS, DEPENDING ON EARNED TIME AND MERITORIOUS TIME, AND THEN BE RELEASED ONTO PRS FOR 12 MONTHS.

IF THE PERSON VIOLATES PRS, HE CAN BE BROUGHT BEFORE THE POST-RELEASE SUPERVISION AND PAROLE COMMISSION IN RALEIGH FOR A VIOLATION HEARING.

FOR SERIOUS VIOLATIONS (NEW CRIMES OR ABSCONDING), THE COMMISSION MAY REVOKE PRS AND ORDER THE PERSON BACK TO PRISON FOR THE TIME REMAINING ON HIS MAXIMUM SENTENCE (THE "EXTRA" 9, 12, OR 60 MONTHS THAT WERE AUTOMATICALLY SET ASIDE AS THE PRS PORTION AT THE BEGINNING OF THE SENTENCE). FOR OTHER VIOLATIONS (MISSED APPOINTMENTS, POSITIVE DRUG SCREENS, ETC.), HE COULD BE RETURNED TO PRISON FOR UP TO 3 MONTHS.

ONCE THE PRS PERIOD EXPIRES OR ALL THE TIME REMAINING ON THE REMAINING TERM OF IMPRISONMENT HAS BEEN SERVED, THE SENTENCE IS COMPLETE.

Jamie Markham is an associate professor of public law and government at the School of Government. He joined the faculty in 2007. His area of interest is criminal law and procedure, with a focus on the law of sentencing and corrections.

Shane Tharrington is the manager of classification and technical support for the prisons division of North Carolina's Department of Public Safety. He has worked in many capacities in the prison system for twenty-five years.

Jason Whitley is a painter, illustrator, and cartoonist. His portrait of Charlotte Hawkins Brown is in the Charlotte Hawkins Brown Museum. His newspaper comic strip, Sea Urchins, is collected into four books.

UNC
SCHOOL OF
GOVERNMENT

IN PRISON

9 781560 118992

ISBN-13: 978-1-56011-899-2

2017.04

This publication was printed and assembled by inmates and staff at the Correction Enterprises Print Plant.

CORRECTION
ENTERPRISES

Not Just Making It Right. Making It Better.

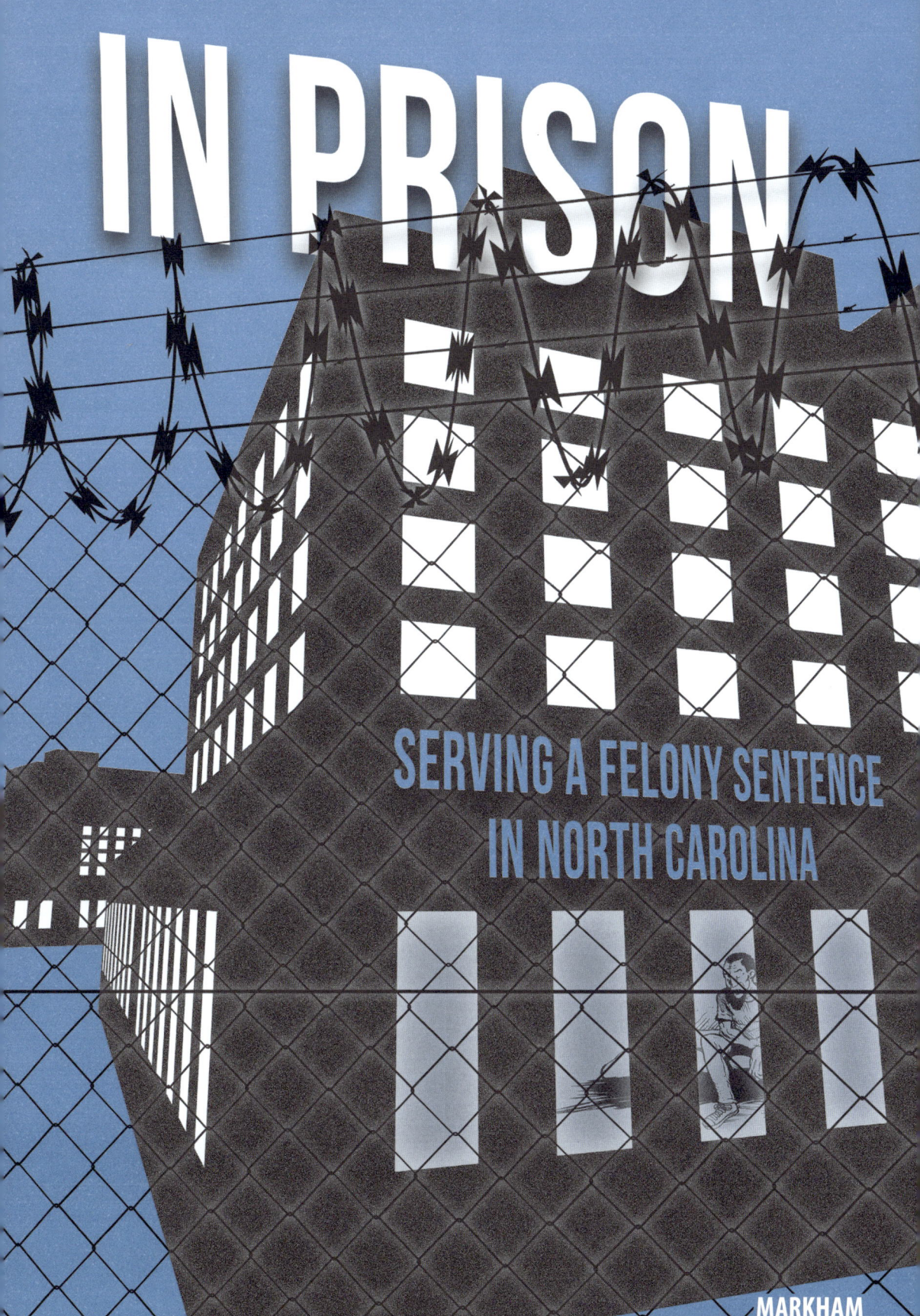

IN PRISON

SERVING A FELONY SENTENCE IN NORTH CAROLINA

MARKHAM
THARRINGTON
WHITLEY

The School of Government at the University of North Carolina at Chapel Hill works to improve the lives of North Carolinians by engaging in practical scholarship that helps public officials and citizens understand and improve state and local government. Established in 1931 as the Institute of Government, the School provides educational, advisory, and research services for state and local governments. The School of Government is also home to a nationally ranked Master of Public Administration program, the North Carolina Judicial College, and specialized centers focused on community and economic development, information technology, and environmental finance.

As the largest university-based local government training, advisory, and research organization in the United States, the School of Government offers up to 200 courses, webinars, and specialized conferences for more than 12,000 public officials each year. In addition, faculty members annually publish approximately 50 books, manuals, reports, articles, bulletins, and other print and online content related to state and local government. The School also produces the *Daily Bulletin Online* each day the General Assembly is in session, reporting on activities for members of the legislature and others who need to follow the course of legislation.

Operating support for the School of Government's programs and activities comes from many sources, including state appropriations, local government membership dues, private contributions, publication sales, course fees, and service contracts.

Visit sog.unc.edu or call 919.966.5381 for more information on the School's courses, publications, programs, and services.

INTRODUCTION

T his short book explains how a felony prison sentence is served in North Carolina. I hope those who read it will gain a better sense of where and how an inmate serves his or her time.

Presenting the information in illustrated form is by no means intended to make light of a very serious subject. It is, rather, offered as an accessible way to fill gaps in knowledge and to address common misperceptions about the way sentences are served. It is meant to give crime victims, defendants, inmates, and their families an understandable resource that translates the words and numbers on a sentencing judgment into a practical reality.

Though the book is of course not a comprehensive legal reference, I hope it will be useful to lawyers and judges, too. An improved understanding of how a sentence is administered should help you advise your clients, negotiate your pleas, and craft your judgments in a way that achieves a more refined measure of justice in each case.

I have neither the technical expertise nor the artistic talent to create something like this on my own. For the former, I relied on co-author Shane Tharrington, classification manager for North Carolina's Division of Adult Correction. For the latter, I turned to Jason Whitley, a talented illustrator who works as a creative lead for instructional innovation at the Eshelman School of Pharmacy at UNC-Chapel Hill. Many thanks to Shane (and to the prison system as a whole) for answering my many questions, and to Jason for turning my stick-figure storyboard into a real graphic novel.

Jamie Markham
Chapel Hill
September 2017

STORY BY
JAMIE MARKHAM AND
SHANE THARRINGTON

ART BY
JASON WHITLEY

1

THE DEFENDANT WILL BE HELD IN THE COUNTY JAIL UNTIL THE PRISON SYSTEM PICKS HIM UP, USUALLY WITHIN A WEEK OR SO.

IF THE DEFENDANT APPEALS HIS SENTENCE, HE COULD BE RELEASED ON AN APPEAL BOND, BUT THAT IS RARE.

THE DEFENDANT'S FIRST STOP WILL BE ONE OF NORTH CAROLINA'S DIAGNOSTIC CENTERS.

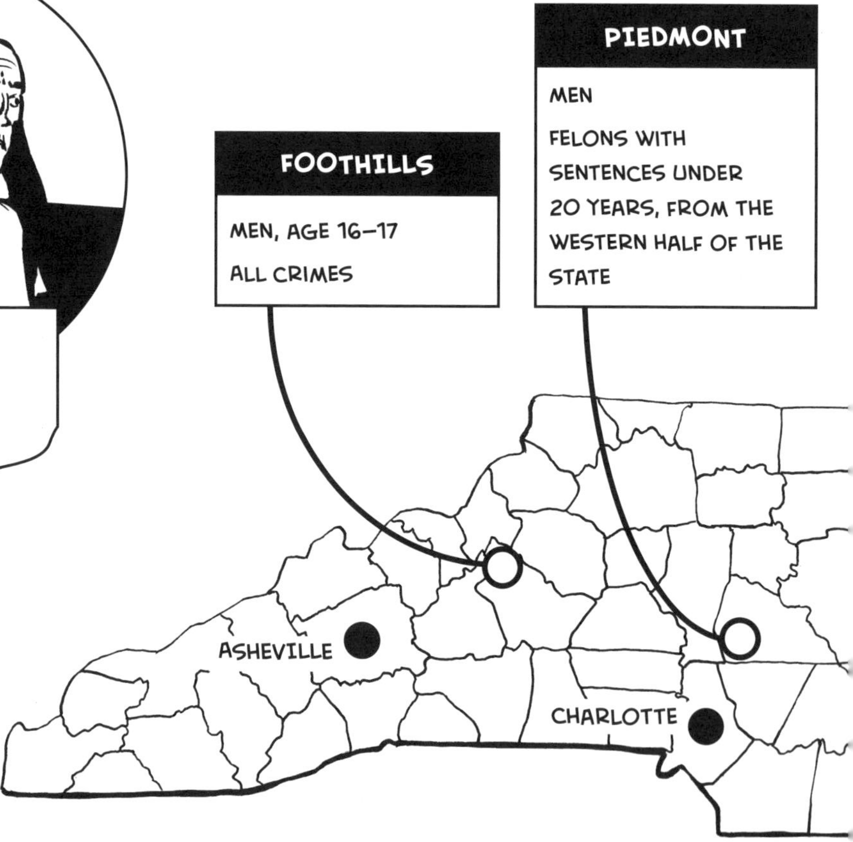

FOOTHILLS

MEN, AGE 16–17

ALL CRIMES

PIEDMONT

MEN

FELONS WITH SENTENCES UNDER 20 YEARS, FROM THE WESTERN HALF OF THE STATE

ASHEVILLE

CHARLOTTE

NORTH CAROLINA'S DIAGNOSTIC CENTERS

THE DEFENDANT GENERALLY WILL GET JAIL CREDIT FOR ALL THE DAYS HE SPENT IN JAIL BEFORE CONVICTION.

JAIL CREDIT IS SUBTRACTED FROM BOTH THE MINIMUM AND MAXIMUM SENTENCE. FOR EXAMPLE, IF THE DEFENDANT HAD 2 MONTHS OF JAIL CREDIT, HE WOULD HAVE 8–19 MONTHS LEFT TO SERVE OF HIS 10–21 MONTH SENTENCE.

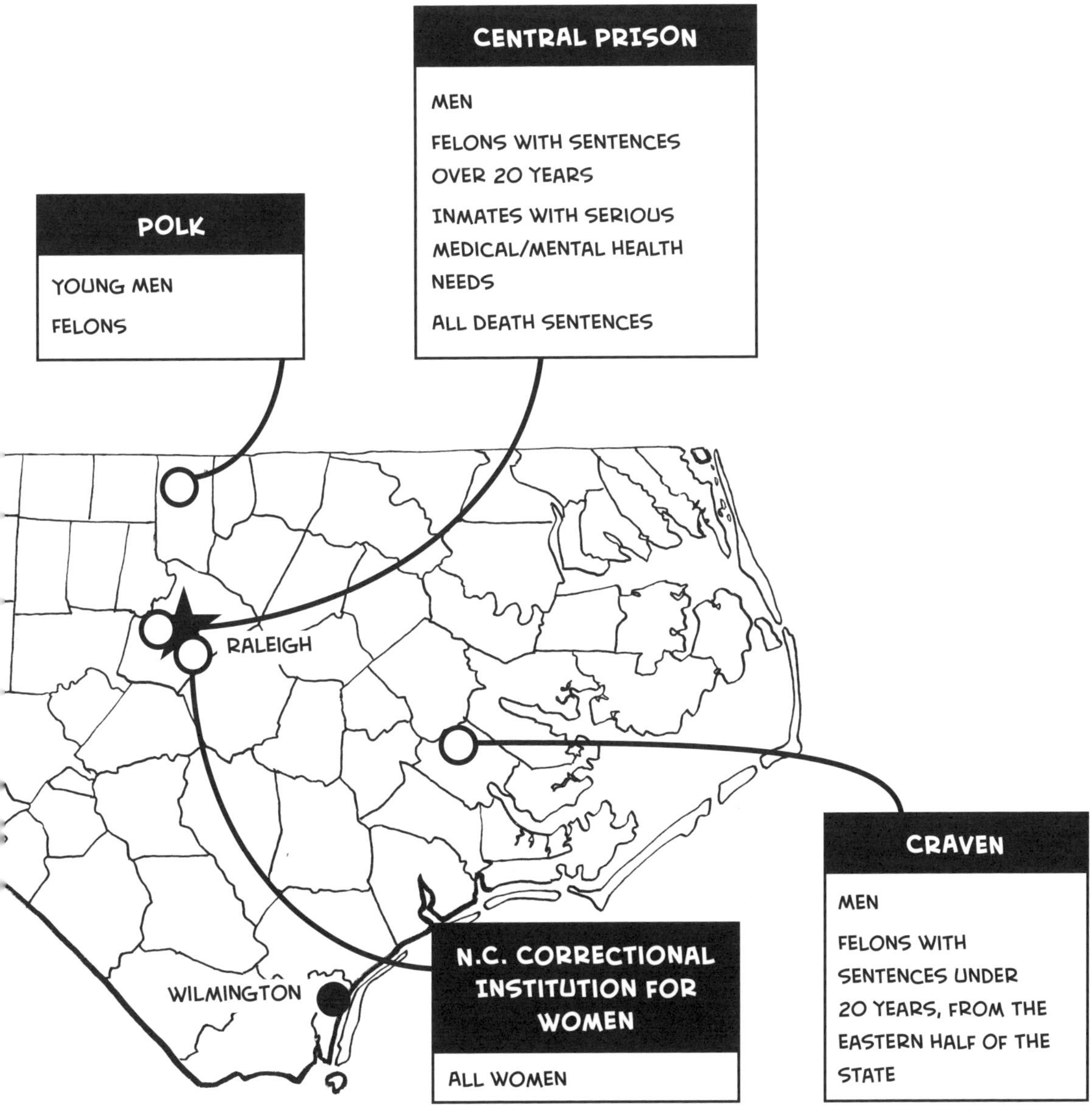

CENTRAL PRISON

MEN

FELONS WITH SENTENCES OVER 20 YEARS

INMATES WITH SERIOUS MEDICAL/MENTAL HEALTH NEEDS

ALL DEATH SENTENCES

POLK

YOUNG MEN

FELONS

RALEIGH

WILMINGTON

CRAVEN

MEN

FELONS WITH SENTENCES UNDER 20 YEARS, FROM THE EASTERN HALF OF THE STATE

N.C. CORRECTIONAL INSTITUTION FOR WOMEN

ALL WOMEN

THE DEFENDANT WILL SPEND 2-4 WEEKS AT THE DIAGNOSTIC FACILITY COMPLETING VARIOUS INPROCESSING ACTIVITES.

CLOTHING EXCHANGE

FINGERPRINTING

RISK-NEEDS ASSESSMENT

DNA SAMPLE

EYE EXAM

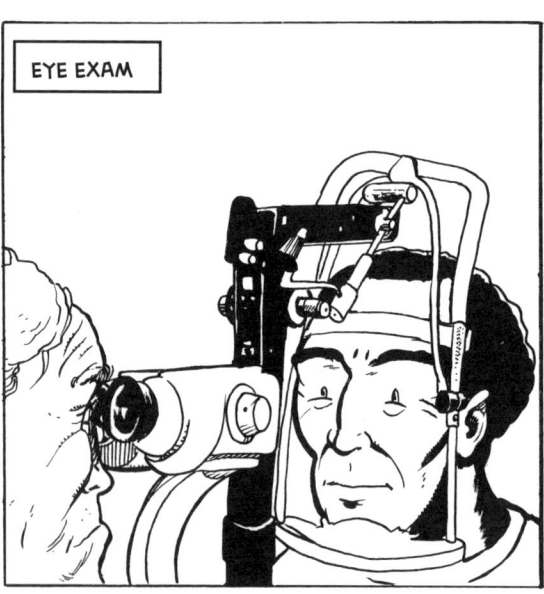

INTELLIGENCE TESTING

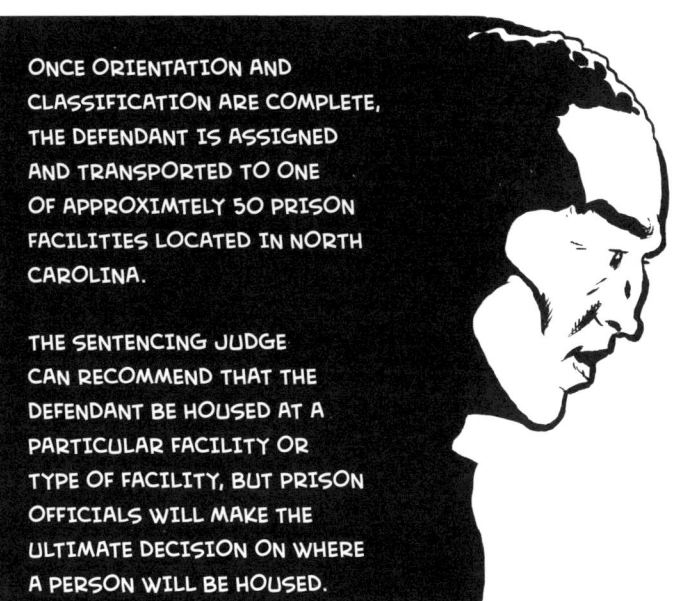

ONCE ORIENTATION AND CLASSIFICATION ARE COMPLETE, THE DEFENDANT IS ASSIGNED AND TRANSPORTED TO ONE OF APPROXIMTELY 50 PRISON FACILITIES LOCATED IN NORTH CAROLINA.

THE SENTENCING JUDGE CAN RECOMMEND THAT THE DEFENDANT BE HOUSED AT A PARTICULAR FACILITY OR TYPE OF FACILITY, BUT PRISON OFFICIALS WILL MAKE THE ULTIMATE DECISION ON WHERE A PERSON WILL BE HOUSED.

THE HOUSING DECISION IS BASED IN PART ON THE CUSTODY LEVEL TO WHICH THE INMATE IS ASSIGNED DURING CLASSIFICATION.

THERE ARE THREE MAIN CUSTODY LEVELS IN THE NORTH CAROLINA PRISON SYSTEM:

CLOSE CUSTODY (MOST SECURE)

MEDIUM CUSTODY

MINIMUM CUSTODY

THE MAP BELOW SHOWS SOME OF THE PRISONS TO WHICH AN INMATE MIGHT BE ASSIGNED. IT HIGHLIGHTS A SAMPLING OF THE SPECIAL PROGRAMS AND JOB ASSIGNMENTS AVAILABLE AT CERTAIN PRISONS. OVER THE COURSE OF SERVING A SENTENCE, SOME INMATES WILL TRANSFER BETWEEN FACILITIES AS CUSTODY LEVELS, WORK ASSIGNMENTS, AND PROGRAM NEEDS CHANGE.

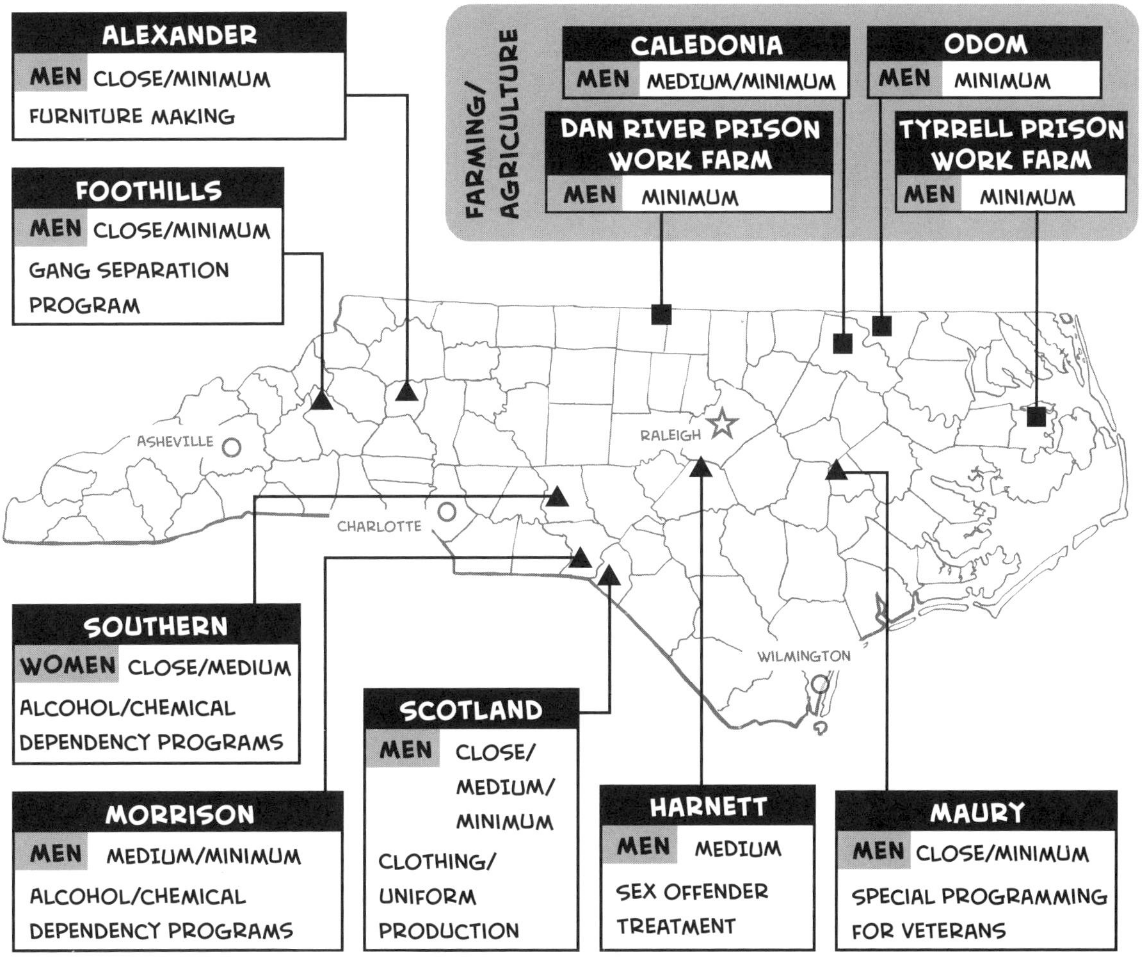

ALEXANDER
MEN CLOSE/MINIMUM
FURNITURE MAKING

FOOTHILLS
MEN CLOSE/MINIMUM
GANG SEPARATION PROGRAM

FARMING/AGRICULTURE

CALEDONIA
MEN MEDIUM/MINIMUM

DAN RIVER PRISON WORK FARM
MEN MINIMUM

ODOM
MEN MINIMUM

TYRRELL PRISON WORK FARM
MEN MINIMUM

ASHEVILLE

RALEIGH ☆

CHARLOTTE

WILMINGTON

SOUTHERN
WOMEN CLOSE/MEDIUM
ALCOHOL/CHEMICAL DEPENDENCY PROGRAMS

MORRISON
MEN MEDIUM/MINIMUM
ALCOHOL/CHEMICAL DEPENDENCY PROGRAMS

SCOTLAND
MEN CLOSE/MEDIUM/MINIMUM
CLOTHING/UNIFORM PRODUCTION

HARNETT
MEN MEDIUM
SEX OFFENDER TREATMENT

MAURY
MEN CLOSE/MINIMUM
SPECIAL PROGRAMMING FOR VETERANS

AT THE ASSIGNED FACILITY, THE INMATE BEGINS SERVING THE REMAINDER OF HIS SENTENCE. HOW LONG IT WILL TAKE TO SERVE IT DEPENDS IN PART ON WHAT HE DOES IN PRISON. PARTICIPATION IN WORK AND PROGRAMS ALLOWS AN INMATE TO EARN SENTENCE CREDITS CALLED **EARNED TIME**.

EARNED TIME IS AWARDED AT DIFFERENT RATES DEPENDING ON THE TYPE OF WORK OR PROGRAM COMPLETED. IN GENERAL, PARTICIPATION IN ANY OF THE JOBS OR PROGRAMS SHOWN BELOW WOULD BE REWARDED WITH 9 DAYS OF EARNED TIME PER MONTH.

EDUCATIONAL PROGRAMS

LAUNDRY

LICENSE PLATES

CONSTRUCTION

CUSTODIAL WORK

AN INMATE AWAITING A WORK OR PROGRAM ASSIGNMENT GENERALLY GETS 3 DAYS OF EARNED TIME PER MONTH.

INMATES CAN ALSO GET ANOTHER CREDIT CALLED **MERITORIOUS TIME** FOR EXEMPLARY ACTS, LIKE WORKING IN BAD WEATHER OR COMPLETING AN EDUCATIONAL DEGREE.

WELDING

ROAD SIGNS

TREATMENT GROUP

DOG TRAINING

ROAD WORK

KITCHEN WORK

SO WHEN IS AN INMATE RELEASED?

FELONY ACTIVE SENTENCES HAVE TWO PARTS: A PERIOD OF CONFINEMENT IN PRISON, FOLLOWED BY A PERIOD OF **POST-RELEASE SUPERVISION** (PRS). PRS IS A PERIOD OF SUPERVISED RELEASE IN THE COMMUNITY, SIMILAR TO PROBATION.

THE LENGTH OF THE PRS PORTION OF THE SENTENCE DEPENDS ON THE INMATE'S CLASS OF OFFENSE AND WHETHER OR NOT THE CRIME REQUIRES REGISTRATION AS A SEX OFFENDER.

OFFENSE CLASS	PRS PORTION OF MAXIMUM
CLASS F–I	9 MONTHS
CLASS B1–E	12 MONTHS
CLASS B1–E SEX CRIME	60 MONTHS

THE PRISON SYSTEM AUTOMATICALLY SUBTRACTS THE PRS PORTION OF THE SENTENCE FROM THE MAXIMUM AND SETS IT OFF TO THE SIDE. THAT'S BECAUSE THE INMATE WILL SERVE THAT TIME ONLY IF HIS POST-RELEASE SUPERVISION IS REVOKED. THE TIME THAT REMAINS AFTER SUBTRACTING THE PRS PORTION IS THE CONFINEMENT PORTION OF THE SENTENCE—THE TIME THE PERSON WILL ACTUALLY SPEND IN PRISON.

⬇ MAXIMUM SENTENCE ⬇

SOME PEOPLE THINK ALL INMATES ARE RELEASED ONCE THEY HAVE SERVED THEIR MINIMUM SENTENCE. **THEY AREN'T.** INSTEAD, THE INMATE STARTS FROM THE MAXIMUM AND WORKS HIS WAY DOWN THROUGH EARNED TIME AND MERITORIOUS TIME.

EXIT

MINIMUM SENTENCE

THE MINIMUM SENTENCE IS JUST THE LOWER LIMIT ON HOW MUCH THE SENTENCE MAY BE REDUCED. IN OTHER WORDS, NO MATTER HOW MUCH WORK HE DOES OR HOW MANY PROGRAMS HE COMPLETES, THE INMATE WILL NOT BE RELEASED BEFORE SERVING HIS MINIMUM SENTENCE.

MOST INMATES ARE NOT ABLE TO WORK THEIR SENTENCES ALL THE WAY DOWN TO THE MINIMUM. AVERAGE RELEASE DATES FOR EACH CLASS OF FELONY ARE SHOWN IN THE TABLE BELOW.

OFFENSE CLASS	PERCENT OF MINIMUM SERVED UPON RELEASE...
CLASS B1–C	102%
CLASS D	103%
CLASS E	104%
CLASS F	105%
CLASS G	107%
CLASS H	114%
CLASS I	113%

NOTICE THAT INMATES WITH MORE SERIOUS CONVICTIONS GENERALLY DO A BETTER JOB OF WORKING THEIR RELEASE DATES DOWN TOWARD THE MINIMUM SENTENCE. WHY? IT'S BECAUSE MANY INMATES WITH SHORTER SENTENCES AREN'T IN PRISON LONG ENOUGH TO COMPLETE PROGRAMS OR GET PLACED IN THE JOBS THAT EARN A LOT OF EARNED TIME.

LET'S PUT IT ALL TOGETHER FOR OUR EXAMPLE OF AN INMATE SERVING A 10–21 MONTH SENTENCE FOR A CLASS G FELONY. THE LAST 9 MONTHS OF HIS SENTENCE WILL BE SET ASIDE FOR PRS, LEAVING 10–12 MONTHS OF CONFINEMENT TO SERVE. ON AVERAGE, AN INMATE WITH A SENTENCE LIKE THAT WILL SERVE 107% OF HIS MINIMUM (10.7 MONTHS IN THIS CASE) BEFORE BEING RELEASED ONTO PRS. THE EARLIEST POSSIBLE RELEASE IS 10 MONTHS. THE LATEST IS 12 MONTHS.

10–12 MONTHS
CONFINEMENT PORTION

9 MONTHS
PRS PORTION

A FELONY INMATE'S SENTENCE IS NOT COMPLETE UPON RELEASE. ALL FELONS SERVE A TERM OF POST-RELEASE SUPERVISION (PRS) AFTER THEY ARE RELEASED FROM PRISON. IT'S MANDATORY—THE INMATE CANNOT REFUSE IT. THE LENGTH OF THE PRS TERM IS GOVERNED BY THE TYPE OF SENTENCE.

OFFENSE CLASS	LENGTH OF PRS
CLASS F–I	9 MONTHS
CLASS B1–E	12 MONTHS
SEX CRIME	60 MONTHS

DURING THE TERM OF PRS, THE PERSON IS SUPERVISED BY A PROBATION/PAROLE OFFICER—THE SAME OFFICERS WHO SUPERVISE PROBATIONERS IN NORTH CAROLINA.

WHAT ABOUT MULTIPLE SENTENCES?

MANY INMATES ARE SERVING TIME FOR MORE THAN ONE CONVICTION.

BY DEFAULT, SENTENCES RUN **CONCURRENTLY**. THAT MEANS THE INMATE SERVES THEM ALL AT ONCE AND GETS RELEASED WHEN THE LONGEST SENTENCE IS COMPLETE.

A JUDGE CAN ORDER **CONSECUTIVE SENTENCES**, SOMETIMES CALLED "BOXCAR" SENTENCES. THAT MEANS ONE SENTENCE DOES NOT BEGIN UNTIL THE ONE BEFORE IT ENDS. THE PRISON SYSTEM COMBINES CONSECUTIVE SENTENCES INTO A SINGLE SENTENCE WITH **ONE POST-RELEASE SUPERVISION PERIOD** AT THE END.

THEY WILL ADD UP ALL THE CONFINEMENT PORTIONS AND THEN ELIMINATE ALL OF THE PRS PORTIONS EXCEPT FOR THE LONGEST ONE. FOR EXAMPLE, IF AN INMATE HAD A 20–36 MONTH SENTENCE FOR A CLASS E FELONY FOLLOWED BY TWO 6–17 MONTH CLASS H FELONY SENTENCES, IT WOULD LOOK LIKE THIS:

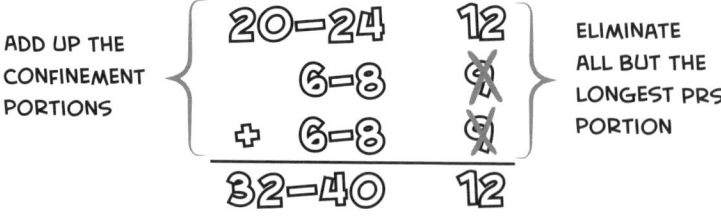

ADD UP THE CONFINEMENT PORTIONS

ELIMINATE ALL BUT THE LONGEST PRS PORTION

THE INMATE WILL SERVE BETWEEN 32 AND 40 MONTHS, DEPENDING ON EARNED TIME AND MERITORIOUS TIME, AND THEN BE RELEASED ONTO PRS FOR 12 MONTHS.

IF THE PERSON VIOLATES PRS, HE CAN BE BROUGHT BEFORE THE POST-RELEASE SUPERVISION AND PAROLE COMMISSION IN RALEIGH FOR A VIOLATION HEARING.

FOR SERIOUS VIOLATIONS (NEW CRIMES OR ABSCONDING), THE COMMISSION MAY REVOKE PRS AND ORDER THE PERSON BACK TO PRISON FOR THE TIME REMAINING ON HIS MAXIMUM SENTENCE (THE "EXTRA" 9, 12, OR 60 MONTHS THAT WERE AUTOMATICALLY SET ASIDE AS THE PRS PORTION AT THE BEGINNING OF THE SENTENCE). FOR OTHER VIOLATIONS (MISSED APPOINTMENTS, POSITIVE DRUG SCREENS, ETC.), HE COULD BE RETURNED TO PRISON FOR UP TO 3 MONTHS.

ONCE THE PRS PERIOD EXPIRES OR ALL THE TIME REMAINING ON THE REMAINING TERM OF IMPRISONMENT HAS BEEN SERVED, THE SENTENCE IS COMPLETE.

Jamie Markham is an associate professor of public law and government at the School of Government. He joined the faculty in 2007. His area of interest is criminal law and procedure, with a focus on the law of sentencing and corrections.

Shane Tharrington is the manager of classification and technical support for the prisons division of North Carolina's Department of Public Safety. He has worked in many capacities in the prison system for twenty-five years.

Jason Whitley is a painter, illustrator, and cartoonist. His portrait of Charlotte Hawkins Brown is in the Charlotte Hawkins Brown Museum. His newspaper comic strip, Sea Urchins, is collected into four books.

This publication was printed and assembled by inmates and staff at the Correction Enterprises Print Plant.

CORRECTION ENTERPRISES

Not Just Making It Right. Making It Better.

ISBN-13: 978-1-56011-899-2

2017.04

IN PRISON

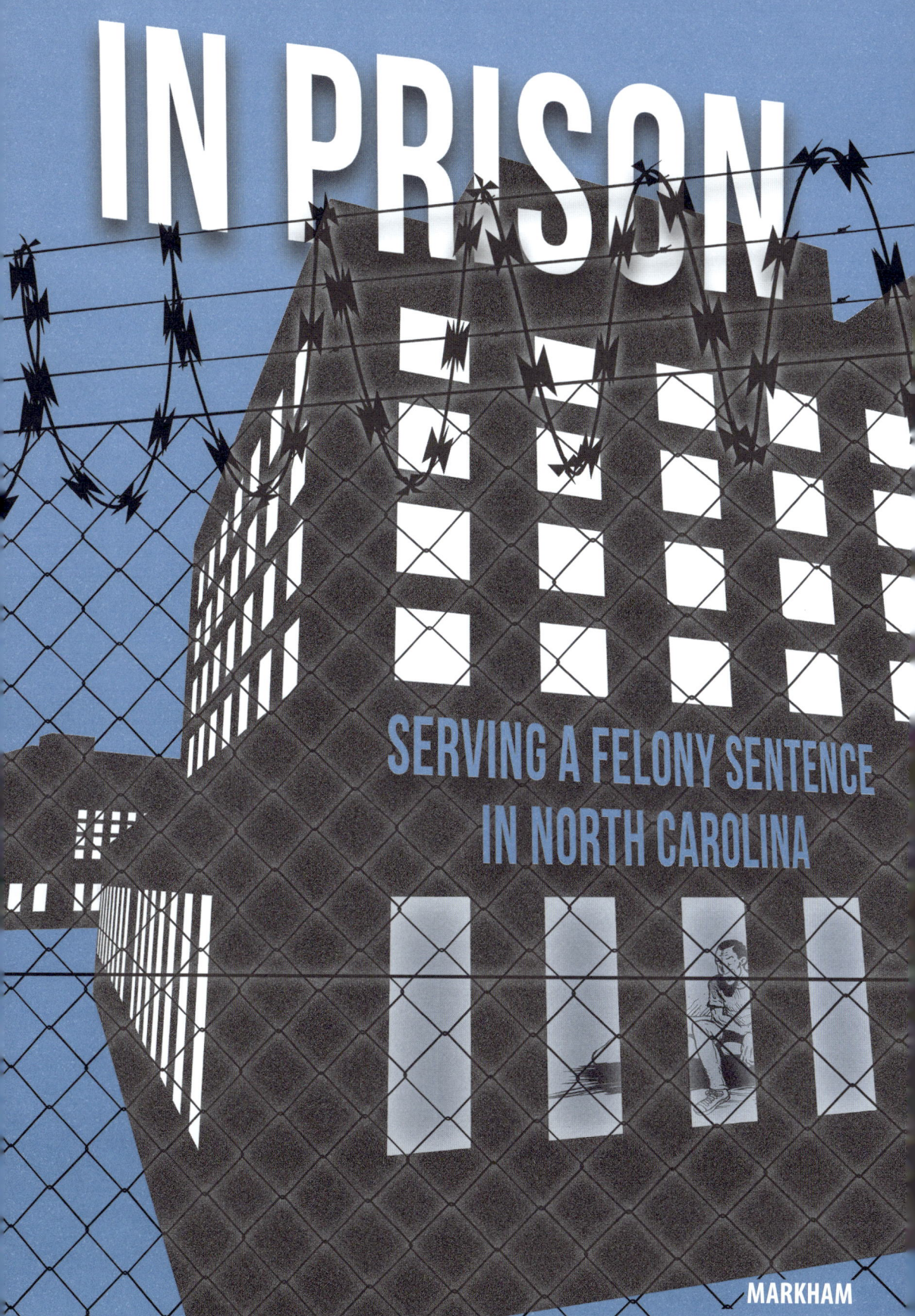

SERVING A FELONY SENTENCE IN NORTH CAROLINA

MARKHAM
THARRINGTON
WHITLEY

The School of Government at the University of North Carolina at Chapel Hill works to improve the lives of North Carolinians by engaging in practical scholarship that helps public officials and citizens understand and improve state and local government. Established in 1931 as the Institute of Government, the School provides educational, advisory, and research services for state and local governments. The School of Government is also home to a nationally ranked Master of Public Administration program, the North Carolina Judicial College, and specialized centers focused on community and economic development, information technology, and environmental finance.

As the largest university-based local government training, advisory, and research organization in the United States, the School of Government offers up to 200 courses, webinars, and specialized conferences for more than 12,000 public officials each year. In addition, faculty members annually publish approximately 50 books, manuals, reports, articles, bulletins, and other print and online content related to state and local government. The School also produces the *Daily Bulletin Online* each day the General Assembly is in session, reporting on activities for members of the legislature and others who need to follow the course of legislation.

Operating support for the School of Government's programs and activities comes from many sources, including state appropriations, local government membership dues, private contributions, publication sales, course fees, and service contracts.

Visit sog.unc.edu or call 919.966.5381 for more information on the School's courses, publications, programs, and services.

INTRODUCTION

T his short book explains how a felony prison sentence is served in North Carolina. I hope those who read it will gain a better sense of where and how an inmate serves his or her time.

Presenting the information in illustrated form is by no means intended to make light of a very serious subject. It is, rather, offered as an accessible way to fill gaps in knowledge and to address common misperceptions about the way sentences are served. It is meant to give crime victims, defendants, inmates, and their families an understandable resource that translates the words and numbers on a sentencing judgment into a practical reality.

Though the book is of course not a comprehensive legal reference, I hope it will be useful to lawyers and judges, too. An improved understanding of how a sentence is administered should help you advise your clients, negotiate your pleas, and craft your judgments in a way that achieves a more refined measure of justice in each case.

I have neither the technical expertise nor the artistic talent to create something like this on my own. For the former, I relied on co-author Shane Tharrington, classification manager for North Carolina's Division of Adult Correction. For the latter, I turned to Jason Whitley, a talented illustrator who works as a creative lead for instructional innovation at the Eshelman School of Pharmacy at UNC-Chapel Hill. Many thanks to Shane (and to the prison system as a whole) for answering my many questions, and to Jason for turning my stick-figure storyboard into a real graphic novel.

Jamie Markham
Chapel Hill
September 2017

STORY BY
JAMIE MARKHAM AND
SHANE THARRINGTON

ART BY
JASON WHITLEY

THE DEFENDANT WILL BE HELD IN THE COUNTY JAIL UNTIL THE PRISON SYSTEM PICKS HIM UP, USUALLY WITHIN A WEEK OR SO.

IF THE DEFENDANT APPEALS HIS SENTENCE, HE COULD BE RELEASED ON AN APPEAL BOND, BUT THAT IS RARE.

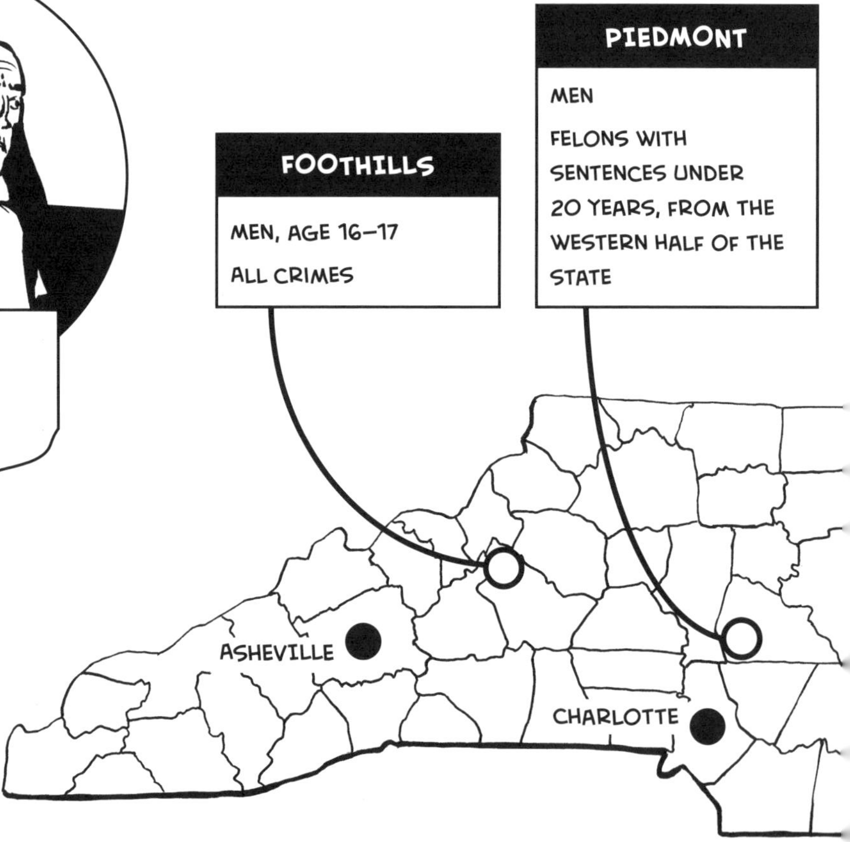

THE DEFENDANT'S FIRST STOP WILL BE ONE OF NORTH CAROLINA'S DIAGNOSTIC CENTERS.

FOOTHILLS

MEN, AGE 16–17
ALL CRIMES

PIEDMONT

MEN

FELONS WITH SENTENCES UNDER 20 YEARS, FROM THE WESTERN HALF OF THE STATE

ASHEVILLE

CHARLOTTE

NORTH CAROLINA'S DIAGNOSTIC CENTERS

THE DEFENDANT GENERALLY WILL GET JAIL CREDIT FOR ALL THE DAYS HE SPENT IN JAIL BEFORE CONVICTION.

JAIL CREDIT IS SUBTRACTED FROM BOTH THE MINIMUM AND MAXIMUM SENTENCE. FOR EXAMPLE, IF THE DEFENDANT HAD 2 MONTHS OF JAIL CREDIT, HE WOULD HAVE 8–19 MONTHS LEFT TO SERVE OF HIS 10–21 MONTH SENTENCE.

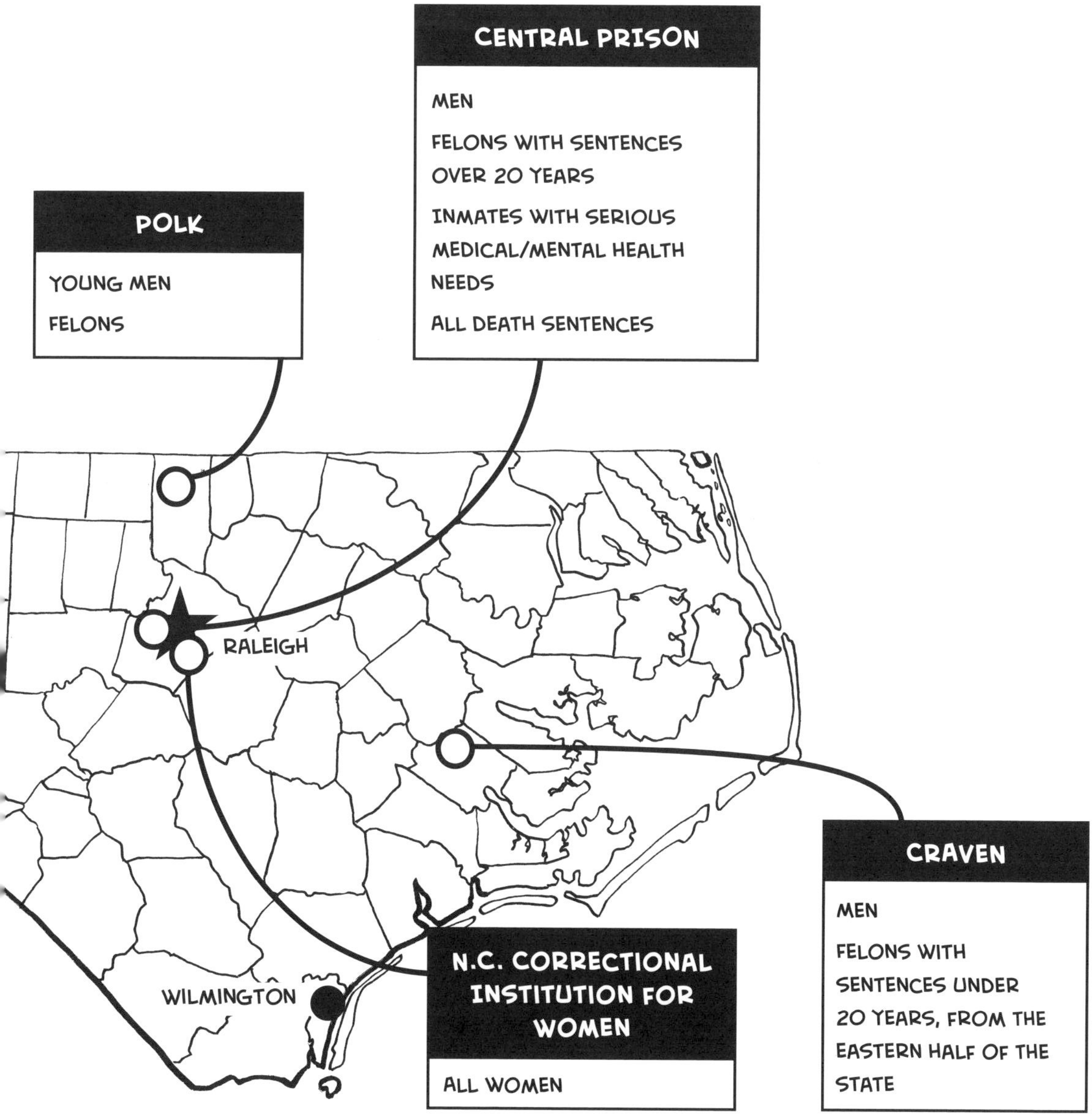

CENTRAL PRISON

MEN

FELONS WITH SENTENCES OVER 20 YEARS

INMATES WITH SERIOUS MEDICAL/MENTAL HEALTH NEEDS

ALL DEATH SENTENCES

POLK

YOUNG MEN

FELONS

RALEIGH

CRAVEN

MEN

FELONS WITH SENTENCES UNDER 20 YEARS, FROM THE EASTERN HALF OF THE STATE

WILMINGTON

N.C. CORRECTIONAL INSTITUTION FOR WOMEN

ALL WOMEN

THE DEFENDANT WILL SPEND 2–4 WEEKS AT THE DIAGNOSTIC FACILITY COMPLETING VARIOUS INPROCESSING ACTIVITES.

CLOTHING EXCHANGE

FINGERPRINTING

RISK-NEEDS ASSESSMENT

DNA SAMPLE

EYE EXAM

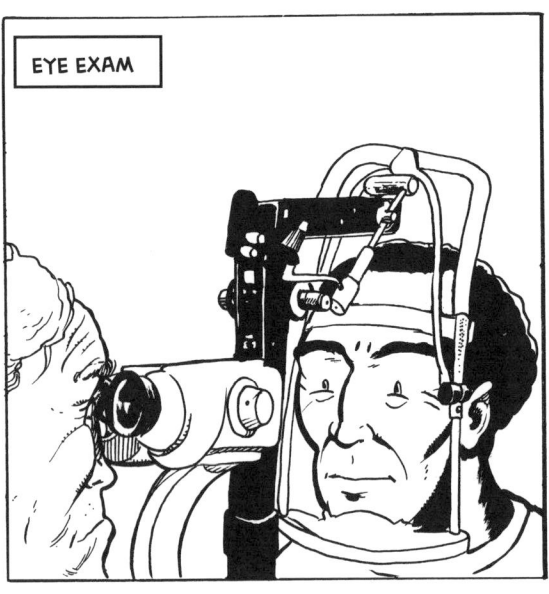

INTELLIGENCE TESTING

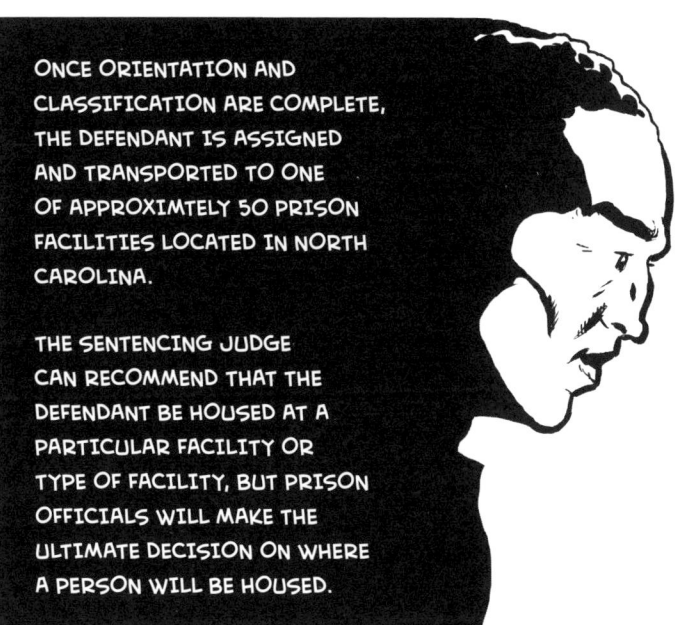

ONCE ORIENTATION AND CLASSIFICATION ARE COMPLETE, THE DEFENDANT IS ASSIGNED AND TRANSPORTED TO ONE OF APPROXIMTELY 50 PRISON FACILITIES LOCATED IN NORTH CAROLINA.

THE SENTENCING JUDGE CAN RECOMMEND THAT THE DEFENDANT BE HOUSED AT A PARTICULAR FACILITY OR TYPE OF FACILITY, BUT PRISON OFFICIALS WILL MAKE THE ULTIMATE DECISION ON WHERE A PERSON WILL BE HOUSED.

THE HOUSING DECISION IS BASED IN PART ON THE CUSTODY LEVEL TO WHICH THE INMATE IS ASSIGNED DURING CLASSIFICATION.

THERE ARE THREE MAIN CUSTODY LEVELS IN THE NORTH CAROLINA PRISON SYSTEM:

CLOSE CUSTODY (MOST SECURE)

MEDIUM CUSTODY

MINIMUM CUSTODY

THE MAP BELOW SHOWS SOME OF THE PRISONS TO WHICH AN INMATE MIGHT BE ASSIGNED. IT HIGHLIGHTS A SAMPLING OF THE SPECIAL PROGRAMS AND JOB ASSIGNMENTS AVAILABLE AT CERTAIN PRISONS. OVER THE COURSE OF SERVING A SENTENCE, SOME INMATES WILL TRANSFER BETWEEN FACILITIES AS CUSTODY LEVELS, WORK ASSIGNMENTS, AND PROGRAM NEEDS CHANGE.

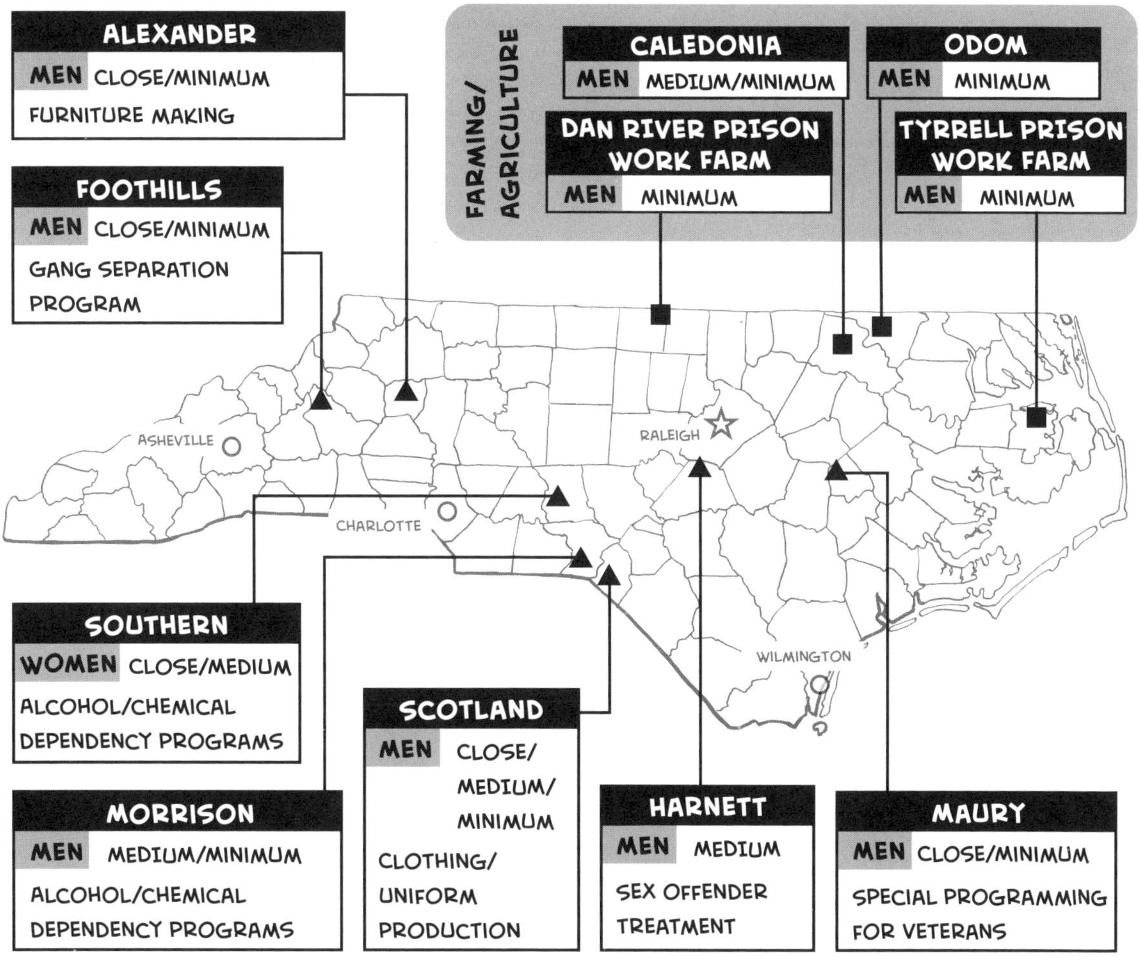

ALEXANDER
MEN CLOSE/MINIMUM
FURNITURE MAKING

FOOTHILLS
MEN CLOSE/MINIMUM
GANG SEPARATION PROGRAM

FARMING/ AGRICULTURE

CALEDONIA
MEN MEDIUM/MINIMUM

DAN RIVER PRISON WORK FARM
MEN MINIMUM

ODOM
MEN MINIMUM

TYRRELL PRISON WORK FARM
MEN MINIMUM

ASHEVILLE

RALEIGH ☆

CHARLOTTE

WILMINGTON

SOUTHERN
WOMEN CLOSE/MEDIUM
ALCOHOL/CHEMICAL DEPENDENCY PROGRAMS

SCOTLAND
MEN CLOSE/ MEDIUM/ MINIMUM
CLOTHING/ UNIFORM PRODUCTION

MORRISON
MEN MEDIUM/MINIMUM
ALCOHOL/CHEMICAL DEPENDENCY PROGRAMS

HARNETT
MEN MEDIUM
SEX OFFENDER TREATMENT

MAURY
MEN CLOSE/MINIMUM
SPECIAL PROGRAMMING FOR VETERANS

AT THE ASSIGNED FACLITY, THE INMATE BEGINS SERVING THE REMAINDER OF HIS SENTENCE. HOW LONG IT WILL TAKE TO SERVE IT DEPENDS IN PART ON WHAT HE DOES IN PRISON. PARTICIPATION IN WORK AND PROGRAMS ALLOWS AN INMATE TO EARN SENTENCE CREDITS CALLED **EARNED TIME**.

EARNED TIME IS AWARDED AT DIFFERENT RATES DEPENDING ON THE TYPE OF WORK OR PROGRAM COMPLETED. IN GENERAL, PARTICIPATION IN ANY OF THE JOBS OR PROGRAMS SHOWN BELOW WOULD BE REWARDED WITH 9 DAYS OF EARNED TIME PER MONTH.

EDUCATIONAL PROGRAMS

LAUNDRY

LICENSE PLATES

CONSTRUCTION

CUSTODIAL WORK

AN INMATE AWAITING A WORK OR PROGRAM ASSIGNMENT GENERALLY GETS 3 DAYS OF EARNED TIME PER MONTH.

INMATES CAN ALSO GET ANOTHER CREDIT CALLED **MERITORIOUS TIME** FOR EXEMPLARY ACTS, LIKE WORKING IN BAD WEATHER OR COMPLETING AN EDUCATIONAL DEGREE.

WELDING

ROAD SIGNS

TREATMENT GROUP

DOG TRAINING

ROAD WORK

KITCHEN WORK

SO WHEN IS AN INMATE RELEASED?

FELONY ACTIVE SENTENCES HAVE TWO PARTS: A PERIOD OF CONFINEMENT IN PRISON, FOLLOWED BY A PERIOD OF **POST-RELEASE SUPERVISION** (PRS). PRS IS A PERIOD OF SUPERVISED RELEASE IN THE COMMUNITY, SIMILAR TO PROBATION.

THE LENGTH OF THE PRS PORTION OF THE SENTENCE DEPENDS ON THE INMATE'S CLASS OF OFFENSE AND WHETHER OR NOT THE CRIME REQUIRES REGISTRATION AS A SEX OFFENDER.

OFFENSE CLASS	PRS PORTION OF MAXIMUM
CLASS F–I	9 MONTHS
CLASS B1–E	12 MONTHS
CLASS B1–E SEX CRIME	60 MONTHS

THE PRISON SYSTEM AUTOMATICALLY SUBTRACTS THE PRS PORTION OF THE SENTENCE FROM THE MAXIMUM AND SETS IT OFF TO THE SIDE. THAT'S BECAUSE THE INMATE WILL SERVE THAT TIME ONLY IF HIS POST-RELEASE SUPERVISION IS REVOKED. THE TIME THAT REMAINS AFTER SUBTRACTING THE PRS PORTION IS THE CONFINEMENT PORTION OF THE SENTENCE—THE TIME THE PERSON WILL ACTUALLY SPEND IN PRISON.

↓ MAXIMUM SENTENCE ↓

SOME PEOPLE THINK ALL INMATES ARE RELEASED ONCE THEY HAVE SERVED THEIR MINIMUM SENTENCE. **THEY AREN'T.** INSTEAD, THE INMATE STARTS FROM THE MAXIMUM AND WORKS HIS WAY DOWN THROUGH EARNED TIME AND MERITORIOUS TIME.

MINIMUM SENTENCE

THE MINIMUM SENTENCE IS JUST THE LOWER LIMIT ON HOW MUCH THE SENTENCE MAY BE REDUCED. IN OTHER WORDS, NO MATTER HOW MUCH WORK HE DOES OR HOW MANY PROGRAMS HE COMPLETES, THE INMATE WILL NOT BE RELEASED BEFORE SERVING HIS MINIMUM SENTENCE.

MOST INMATES ARE NOT ABLE TO WORK THEIR SENTENCES ALL THE WAY DOWN TO THE MINIMUM. AVERAGE RELEASE DATES FOR EACH CLASS OF FELONY ARE SHOWN IN THE TABLE BELOW.

OFFENSE CLASS	PERCENT OF MINIMUM SERVED UPON RELEASE...
CLASS B1–C	102%
CLASS D	103%
CLASS E	104%
CLASS F	105%
CLASS G	107%
CLASS H	114%
CLASS I	113%

NOTICE THAT INMATES WITH MORE SERIOUS CONVICTIONS GENERALLY DO A BETTER JOB OF WORKING THEIR RELEASE DATES DOWN TOWARD THE MINIMUM SENTENCE. WHY? IT'S BECAUSE MANY INMATES WITH SHORTER SENTENCES AREN'T IN PRISON LONG ENOUGH TO COMPLETE PROGRAMS OR GET PLACED IN THE JOBS THAT EARN A LOT OF EARNED TIME.

LET'S PUT IT ALL TOGETHER FOR OUR EXAMPLE OF AN INMATE SERVING A 10–21 MONTH SENTENCE FOR A CLASS G FELONY. THE LAST 9 MONTHS OF HIS SENTENCE WILL BE SET ASIDE FOR PRS, LEAVING 10–12 MONTHS OF CONFINEMENT TO SERVE. ON AVERAGE, AN INMATE WITH A SENTENCE LIKE THAT WILL SERVE 107% OF HIS MINIMUM (10.7 MONTHS IN THIS CASE) BEFORE BEING RELEASED ONTO PRS. THE EARLIEST POSSIBLE RELEASE IS 10 MONTHS. THE LATEST IS 12 MONTHS.

10-12 MONTHS

CONFINEMENT PORTION

9 MONTHS

PRS PORTION

A FELONY INMATE'S SENTENCE IS NOT COMPLETE UPON RELEASE. ALL FELONS SERVE A TERM OF POST-RELEASE SUPERVISION (PRS) AFTER THEY ARE RELEASED FROM PRISON. IT'S MANDATORY—THE INMATE CANNOT REFUSE IT. THE LENGTH OF THE PRS TERM IS GOVERNED BY THE TYPE OF SENTENCE.

OFFENSE CLASS	LENGTH OF PRS
CLASS F–I	9 MONTHS
CLASS B1–E	12 MONTHS
SEX CRIME	60 MONTHS

DURING THE TERM OF PRS, THE PERSON IS SUPERVISED BY A PROBATION/PAROLE OFFICER—THE SAME OFFICERS WHO SUPERVISE PROBATIONERS IN NORTH CAROLINA.

WHAT ABOUT MULTIPLE SENTENCES?

MANY INMATES ARE SERVING TIME FOR MORE THAN ONE CONVICTION.

BY DEFAULT, SENTENCES RUN **CONCURRENTLY**. THAT MEANS THE INMATE SERVES THEM ALL AT ONCE AND GETS RELEASED WHEN THE LONGEST SENTENCE IS COMPLETE.

A JUDGE CAN ORDER **CONSECUTIVE SENTENCES**, SOMETIMES CALLED "BOXCAR" SENTENCES. THAT MEANS ONE SENTENCE DOES NOT BEGIN UNTIL THE ONE BEFORE IT ENDS. THE PRISON SYSTEM COMBINES CONSECUTIVE SENTENCES INTO A SINGLE SENTENCE WITH **ONE POST-RELEASE SUPERVISION PERIOD** AT THE END.

THEY WILL ADD UP ALL THE CONFINEMENT PORTIONS AND THEN ELIMINATE ALL OF THE PRS PORTIONS EXCEPT FOR THE LONGEST ONE. FOR EXAMPLE, IF AN INMATE HAD A 20–36 MONTH SENTENCE FOR A CLASS E FELONY FOLLOWED BY TWO 6–17 MONTH CLASS H FELONY SENTENCES, IT WOULD LOOK LIKE THIS:

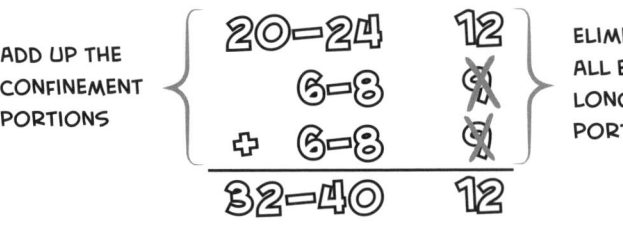

ADD UP THE CONFINEMENT PORTIONS

ELIMINATE ALL BUT THE LONGEST PRS PORTION

THE INMATE WILL SERVE BETWEEN 32 AND 40 MONTHS, DEPENDING ON EARNED TIME AND MERITORIOUS TIME, AND THEN BE RELEASED ONTO PRS FOR 12 MONTHS.

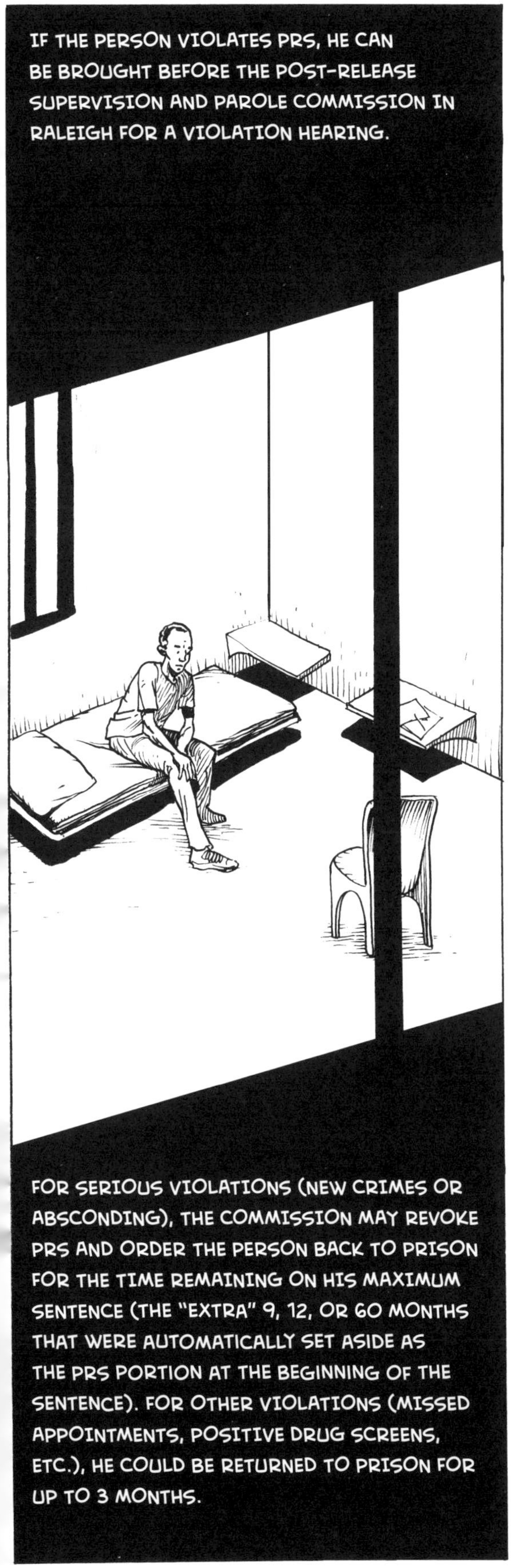

IF THE PERSON VIOLATES PRS, HE CAN BE BROUGHT BEFORE THE POST-RELEASE SUPERVISION AND PAROLE COMMISSION IN RALEIGH FOR A VIOLATION HEARING.

ONCE THE PRS PERIOD EXPIRES OR ALL THE TIME REMAINING ON THE REMAINING TERM OF IMPRISONMENT HAS BEEN SERVED, THE SENTENCE IS COMPLETE.

FOR SERIOUS VIOLATIONS (NEW CRIMES OR ABSCONDING), THE COMMISSION MAY REVOKE PRS AND ORDER THE PERSON BACK TO PRISON FOR THE TIME REMAINING ON HIS MAXIMUM SENTENCE (THE "EXTRA" 9, 12, OR 60 MONTHS THAT WERE AUTOMATICALLY SET ASIDE AS THE PRS PORTION AT THE BEGINNING OF THE SENTENCE). FOR OTHER VIOLATIONS (MISSED APPOINTMENTS, POSITIVE DRUG SCREENS, ETC.), HE COULD BE RETURNED TO PRISON FOR UP TO 3 MONTHS.

Jamie Markham is an associate professor of public law and government at the School of Government. He joined the faculty in 2007. His area of interest is criminal law and procedure, with a focus on the law of sentencing and corrections.

Shane Tharrington is the manager of classification and technical support for the prisons division of North Carolina's Department of Public Safety. He has worked in many capacities in the prison system for twenty-five years.

Jason Whitley is a painter, illustrator, and cartoonist. His portrait of Charlotte Hawkins Brown is in the Charlotte Hawkins Brown Museum. His newspaper comic strip, Sea Urchins, is collected into four books.

UNC
SCHOOL OF
GOVERNMENT

This publication was printed and assembled by inmates and staff at the Correction Enterprises Print Plant.

CORRECTION
ENTERPRISES
Not Just Making It Right. Making It Better.

ISBN-13: 978-1-56011-899-2
2017.04

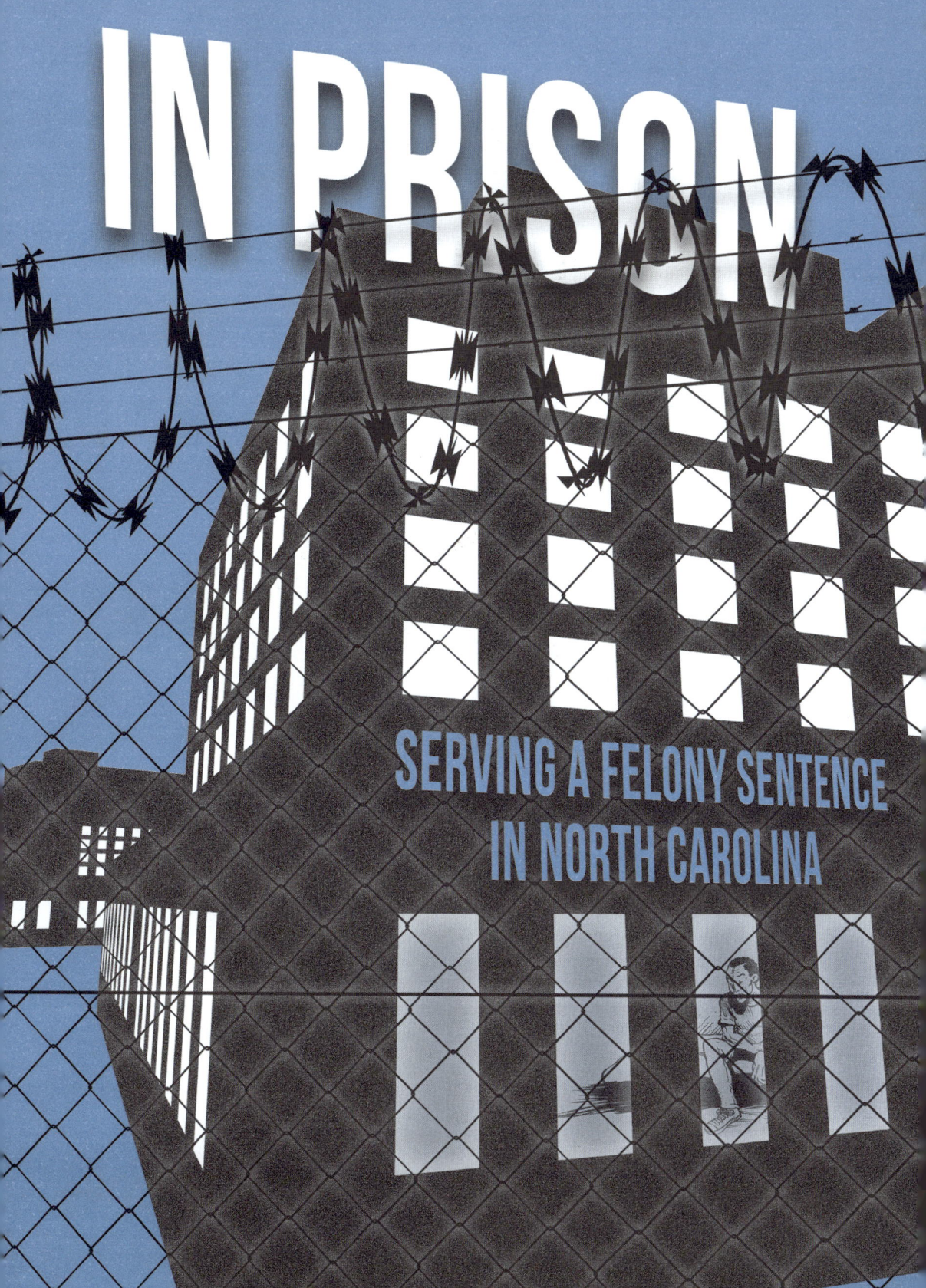

IN PRISON

SERVING A FELONY SENTENCE IN NORTH CAROLINA

MARKHAM
THARRINGTON
WHITLEY

The School of Government at the University of North Carolina at Chapel Hill works to improve the lives of North Carolinians by engaging in practical scholarship that helps public officials and citizens understand and improve state and local government. Established in 1931 as the Institute of Government, the School provides educational, advisory, and research services for state and local governments. The School of Government is also home to a nationally ranked Master of Public Administration program, the North Carolina Judicial College, and specialized centers focused on community and economic development, information technology, and environmental finance.

As the largest university-based local government training, advisory, and research organization in the United States, the School of Government offers up to 200 courses, webinars, and specialized conferences for more than 12,000 public officials each year. In addition, faculty members annually publish approximately 50 books, manuals, reports, articles, bulletins, and other print and online content related to state and local government. The School also produces the *Daily Bulletin Online* each day the General Assembly is in session, reporting on activities for members of the legislature and others who need to follow the course of legislation.

Operating support for the School of Government's programs and activities comes from many sources, including state appropriations, local government membership dues, private contributions, publication sales, course fees, and service contracts.

Visit sog.unc.edu or call 919.966.5381 for more information on the School's courses, publications, programs, and services.

© 2017
School of Government
The University of North Carolina at Chapel Hill

Printed in the United States of America

21 20 19 18 17   1 2 3 4 5

ISBN 978-1-56011-899-2

⊚ This publication is printed on permanent, acid-free paper in compliance with the North Carolina General Statutes.

♲ Printed on recycled paper

INTRODUCTION

This short book explains how a felony prison sentence is served in North Carolina. I hope those who read it will gain a better sense of where and how an inmate serves his or her time.

Presenting the information in illustrated form is by no means intended to make light of a very serious subject. It is, rather, offered as an accessible way to fill gaps in knowledge and to address common misperceptions about the way sentences are served. It is meant to give crime victims, defendants, inmates, and their families an understandable resource that translates the words and numbers on a sentencing judgment into a practical reality.

Though the book is of course not a comprehensive legal reference, I hope it will be useful to lawyers and judges, too. An improved understanding of how a sentence is administered should help you advise your clients, negotiate your pleas, and craft your judgments in a way that achieves a more refined measure of justice in each case.

I have neither the technical expertise nor the artistic talent to create something like this on my own. For the former, I relied on co-author Shane Tharrington, classification manager for North Carolina's Division of Adult Correction. For the latter, I turned to Jason Whitley, a talented illustrator who works as a creative lead for instructional innovation at the Eshelman School of Pharmacy at UNC-Chapel Hill. Many thanks to Shane (and to the prison system as a whole) for answering my many questions, and to Jason for turning my stick-figure storyboard into a real graphic novel.

Jamie Markham
Chapel Hill
September 2017

THE DEFENDANT WILL BE HELD IN THE COUNTY JAIL UNTIL THE PRISON SYSTEM PICKS HIM UP, USUALLY WITHIN A WEEK OR SO.

IF THE DEFENDANT APPEALS HIS SENTENCE, HE COULD BE RELEASED ON AN APPEAL BOND, BUT THAT IS RARE.

THE DEFENDANT'S FIRST STOP WILL BE ONE OF NORTH CAROLINA'S DIAGNOSTIC CENTERS.

FOOTHILLS

MEN, AGE 16–17

ALL CRIMES

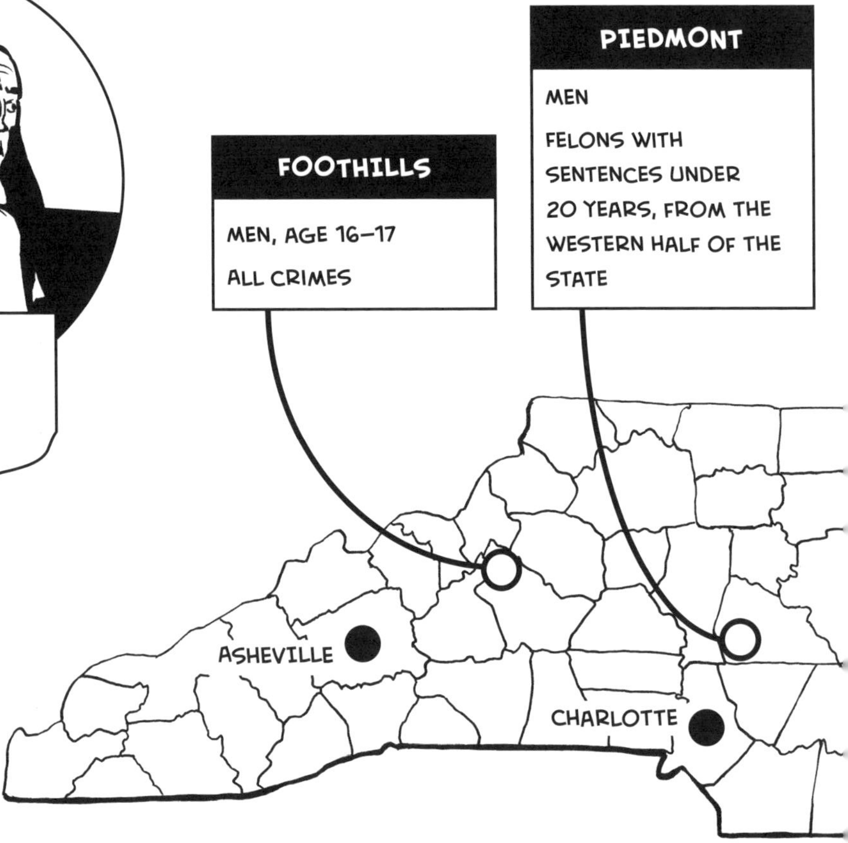

PIEDMONT

MEN

FELONS WITH SENTENCES UNDER 20 YEARS, FROM THE WESTERN HALF OF THE STATE

ASHEVILLE

CHARLOTTE

NORTH CAROLINA'S DIAGNOSTIC CENTERS

THE DEFENDANT GENERALLY WILL GET JAIL CREDIT FOR ALL THE DAYS HE SPENT IN JAIL BEFORE CONVICTION.

JAIL CREDIT IS SUBTRACTED FROM BOTH THE MINIMUM AND MAXIMUM SENTENCE. FOR EXAMPLE, IF THE DEFENDANT HAD 2 MONTHS OF JAIL CREDIT, HE WOULD HAVE 8–19 MONTHS LEFT TO SERVE OF HIS 10–21 MONTH SENTENCE.

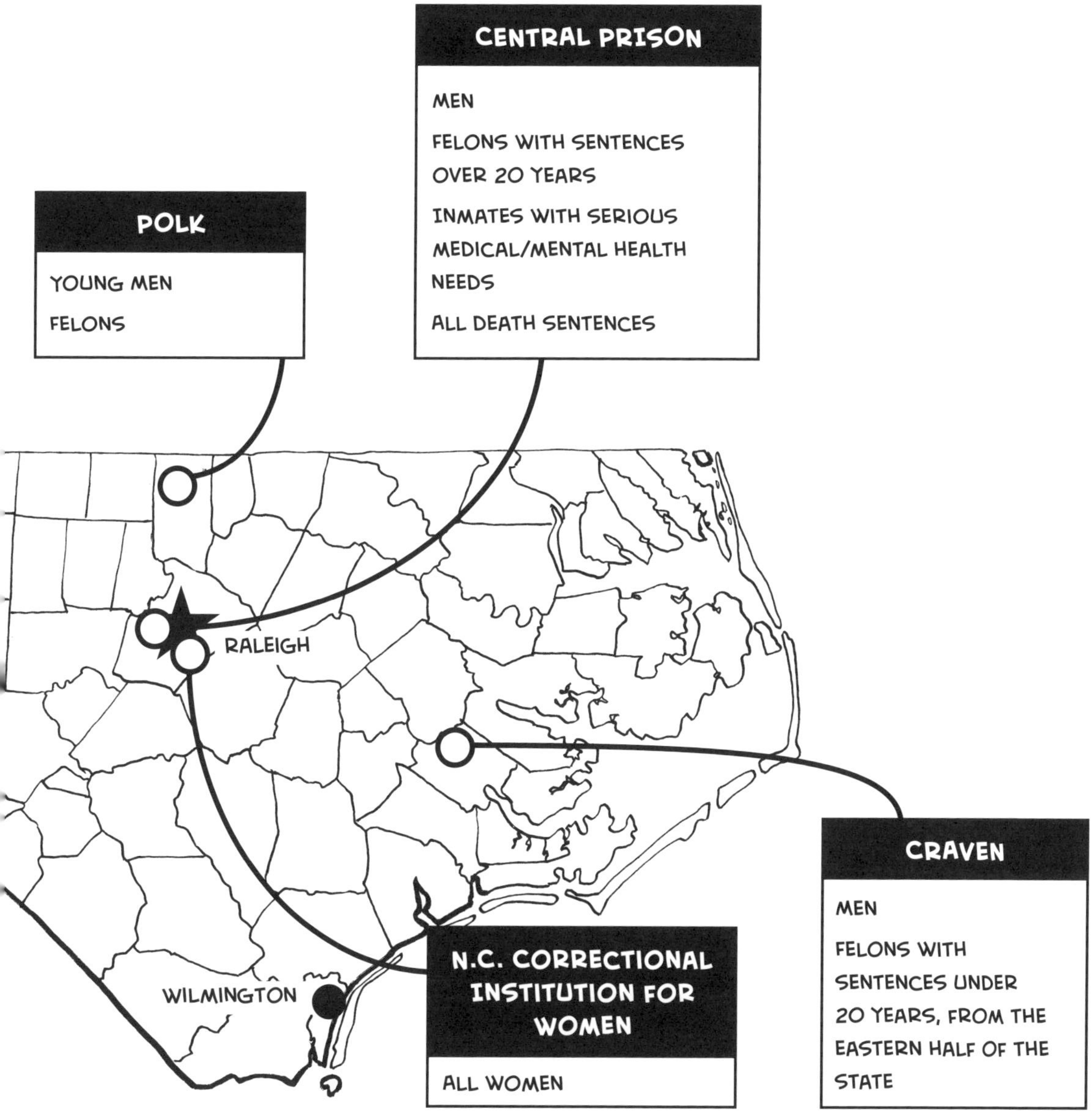

CENTRAL PRISON

MEN

FELONS WITH SENTENCES OVER 20 YEARS

INMATES WITH SERIOUS MEDICAL/MENTAL HEALTH NEEDS

ALL DEATH SENTENCES

POLK

YOUNG MEN

FELONS

RALEIGH

CRAVEN

MEN

FELONS WITH SENTENCES UNDER 20 YEARS, FROM THE EASTERN HALF OF THE STATE

WILMINGTON

N.C. CORRECTIONAL INSTITUTION FOR WOMEN

ALL WOMEN

THE DEFENDANT WILL SPEND 2–4 WEEKS AT THE DIAGNOSTIC FACILITY COMPLETING VARIOUS INPROCESSING ACTIVITES.

CLOTHING EXCHANGE

FINGERPRINTING

RISK-NEEDS ASSESSMENT

DNA SAMPLE

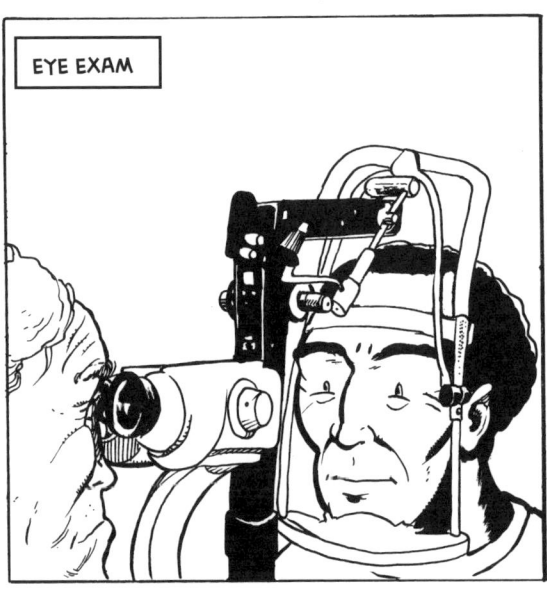

EYE EXAM

INTELLIGENCE TESTING

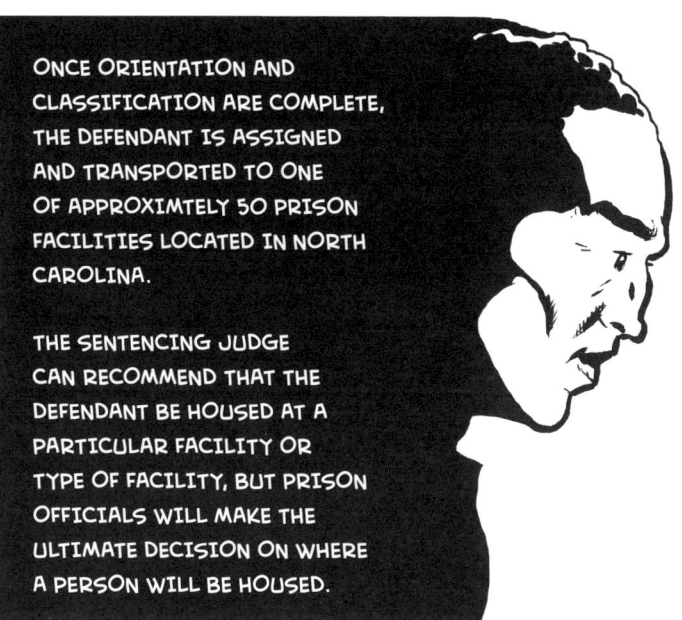

ONCE ORIENTATION AND CLASSIFICATION ARE COMPLETE, THE DEFENDANT IS ASSIGNED AND TRANSPORTED TO ONE OF APPROXIMTELY 50 PRISON FACILITIES LOCATED IN NORTH CAROLINA.

THE SENTENCING JUDGE CAN RECOMMEND THAT THE DEFENDANT BE HOUSED AT A PARTICULAR FACILITY OR TYPE OF FACILITY, BUT PRISON OFFICIALS WILL MAKE THE ULTIMATE DECISION ON WHERE A PERSON WILL BE HOUSED.

THE HOUSING DECISION IS BASED IN PART ON THE CUSTODY LEVEL TO WHICH THE INMATE IS ASSIGNED DURING CLASSIFICATION.

THERE ARE THREE MAIN CUSTODY LEVELS IN THE NORTH CAROLINA PRISON SYSTEM:

CLOSE CUSTODY (MOST SECURE)

MEDIUM CUSTODY

MINIMUM CUSTODY

THE MAP BELOW SHOWS SOME OF THE PRISONS TO WHICH AN INMATE MIGHT BE ASSIGNED. IT HIGHLIGHTS A SAMPLING OF THE SPECIAL PROGRAMS AND JOB ASSIGNMENTS AVAILABLE AT CERTAIN PRISONS. OVER THE COURSE OF SERVING A SENTENCE, SOME INMATES WILL TRANSFER BETWEEN FACILITIES AS CUSTODY LEVELS, WORK ASSIGNMENTS, AND PROGRAM NEEDS CHANGE.

ALEXANDER
MEN CLOSE/MINIMUM
FURNITURE MAKING

FOOTHILLS
MEN CLOSE/MINIMUM
GANG SEPARATION PROGRAM

FARMING/AGRICULTURE

CALEDONIA
MEN MEDIUM/MINIMUM

DAN RIVER PRISON WORK FARM
MEN MINIMUM

ODOM
MEN MINIMUM

TYRRELL PRISON WORK FARM
MEN MINIMUM

ASHEVILLE

RALEIGH

CHARLOTTE

WILMINGTON

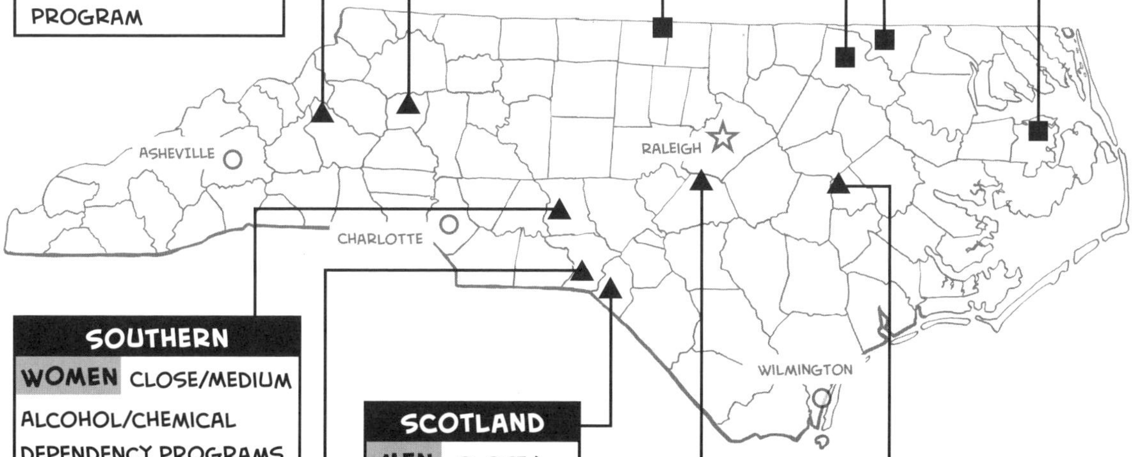

SOUTHERN
WOMEN CLOSE/MEDIUM
ALCOHOL/CHEMICAL DEPENDENCY PROGRAMS

MORRISON
MEN MEDIUM/MINIMUM
ALCOHOL/CHEMICAL DEPENDENCY PROGRAMS

SCOTLAND
MEN CLOSE/MEDIUM/MINIMUM
CLOTHING/UNIFORM PRODUCTION

HARNETT
MEN MEDIUM
SEX OFFENDER TREATMENT

MAURY
MEN CLOSE/MINIMUM
SPECIAL PROGRAMMING FOR VETERANS

AT THE ASSIGNED FACLITY, THE INMATE BEGINS SERVING THE REMAINDER OF HIS SENTENCE. HOW LONG IT WILL TAKE TO SERVE IT DEPENDS IN PART ON WHAT HE DOES IN PRISON. PARTICIPATION IN WORK AND PROGRAMS ALLOWS AN INMATE TO EARN SENTENCE CREDITS CALLED **EARNED TIME**.

EARNED TIME IS AWARDED AT DIFFERENT RATES DEPENDING ON THE TYPE OF WORK OR PROGRAM COMPLETED. IN GENERAL, PARTICIPATION IN ANY OF THE JOBS OR PROGRAMS SHOWN BELOW WOULD BE REWARDED WITH 9 DAYS OF EARNED TIME PER MONTH.

EDUCATIONAL PROGRAMS

LAUNDRY

LICENSE PLATES

CONSTRUCTION

CUSTODIAL WORK

AN INMATE AWAITING A WORK OR PROGRAM ASSIGNMENT GENERALLY GETS 3 DAYS OF EARNED TIME PER MONTH.

INMATES CAN ALSO GET ANOTHER CREDIT CALLED **MERITORIOUS TIME** FOR EXEMPLARY ACTS, LIKE WORKING IN BAD WEATHER OR COMPLETING AN EDUCATIONAL DEGREE.

WELDING

ROAD SIGNS

TREATMENT GROUP

DOG TRAINING

ROAD WORK

KITCHEN WORK

SO WHEN IS AN INMATE RELEASED?

FELONY ACTIVE SENTENCES HAVE TWO PARTS: A PERIOD OF CONFINEMENT IN PRISON, FOLLOWED BY A PERIOD OF **POST-RELEASE SUPERVISION** (PRS). PRS IS A PERIOD OF SUPERVISED RELEASE IN THE COMMUNITY, SIMILAR TO PROBATION.

THE LENGTH OF THE PRS PORTION OF THE SENTENCE DEPENDS ON THE INMATE'S CLASS OF OFFENSE AND WHETHER OR NOT THE CRIME REQUIRES REGISTRATION AS A SEX OFFENDER.

OFFENSE CLASS	PRS PORTION OF MAXIMUM
CLASS F–I	9 MONTHS
CLASS B1–E	12 MONTHS
CLASS B1–E SEX CRIME	60 MONTHS

THE PRISON SYSTEM AUTOMATICALLY SUBTRACTS THE PRS PORTION OF THE SENTENCE FROM THE MAXIMUM AND SETS IT OFF TO THE SIDE. THAT'S BECAUSE THE INMATE WILL SERVE THAT TIME ONLY IF HIS POST-RELEASE SUPERVISION IS REVOKED. THE TIME THAT REMAINS AFTER SUBTRACTING THE PRS PORTION IS THE CONFINEMENT PORTION OF THE SENTENCE—THE TIME THE PERSON WILL ACTUALLY SPEND IN PRISON.

⬇ MAXIMUM SENTENCE ⬇

SOME PEOPLE THINK ALL INMATES ARE RELEASED ONCE THEY HAVE SERVED THEIR MINIMUM SENTENCE. **THEY AREN'T**. INSTEAD, THE INMATE STARTS FROM THE MAXIMUM AND WORKS HIS WAY DOWN THROUGH EARNED TIME AND MERITORIOUS TIME.

EXIT

MINIMUM SENTENCE

THE MINIMUM SENTENCE IS JUST THE LOWER LIMIT ON HOW MUCH THE SENTENCE MAY BE REDUCED. IN OTHER WORDS, NO MATTER HOW MUCH WORK HE DOES OR HOW MANY PROGRAMS HE COMPLETES, THE INMATE WILL NOT BE RELEASED BEFORE SERVING HIS MINIMUM SENTENCE.

MOST INMATES ARE NOT ABLE TO WORK THEIR SENTENCES ALL THE WAY DOWN TO THE MINIMUM. AVERAGE RELEASE DATES FOR EACH CLASS OF FELONY ARE SHOWN IN THE TABLE BELOW.

OFFENSE CLASS	PERCENT OF MINIMUM SERVED UPON RELEASE...
CLASS B1–C	102%
CLASS D	103%
CLASS E	104%
CLASS F	105%
CLASS G	107%
CLASS H	114%
CLASS I	113%

NOTICE THAT INMATES WITH MORE SERIOUS CONVICTIONS GENERALLY DO A BETTER JOB OF WORKING THEIR RELEASE DATES DOWN TOWARD THE MINIMUM SENTENCE. WHY? IT'S BECAUSE MANY INMATES WITH SHORTER SENTENCES AREN'T IN PRISON LONG ENOUGH TO COMPLETE PROGRAMS OR GET PLACED IN THE JOBS THAT EARN A LOT OF EARNED TIME.

LET'S PUT IT ALL TOGETHER FOR OUR EXAMPLE OF AN INMATE SERVING A 10–21 MONTH SENTENCE FOR A CLASS G FELONY. THE LAST 9 MONTHS OF HIS SENTENCE WILL BE SET ASIDE FOR PRS, LEAVING 10–12 MONTHS OF CONFINEMENT TO SERVE. ON AVERAGE, AN INMATE WITH A SENTENCE LIKE THAT WILL SERVE 107% OF HIS MINIMUM (10.7 MONTHS IN THIS CASE) BEFORE BEING RELEASED ONTO PRS. THE EARLIEST POSSIBLE RELEASE IS 10 MONTHS. THE LATEST IS 12 MONTHS.

10-12 MONTHS

CONFINEMENT PORTION

9 MONTHS

PRS PORTION

A FELONY INMATE'S SENTENCE IS NOT COMPLETE UPON RELEASE. ALL FELONS SERVE A TERM OF POST-RELEASE SUPERVISION (PRS) AFTER THEY ARE RELEASED FROM PRISON. IT'S MANDATORY—THE INMATE CANNOT REFUSE IT. THE LENGTH OF THE PRS TERM IS GOVERNED BY THE TYPE OF SENTENCE.

OFFENSE CLASS	LENGTH OF PRS
CLASS F-I	9 MONTHS
CLASS B1-E	12 MONTHS
SEX CRIME	60 MONTHS

DURING THE TERM OF PRS, THE PERSON IS SUPERVISED BY A PROBATION/PAROLE OFFICER—THE SAME OFFICERS WHO SUPERVISE PROBATIONERS IN NORTH CAROLINA.

WHAT ABOUT MULTIPLE SENTENCES?

MANY INMATES ARE SERVING TIME FOR MORE THAN ONE CONVICTION.

BY DEFAULT, SENTENCES RUN **CONCURRENTLY**. THAT MEANS THE INMATE SERVES THEM ALL AT ONCE AND GETS RELEASED WHEN THE LONGEST SENTENCE IS COMPLETE.

A JUDGE CAN ORDER **CONSECUTIVE SENTENCES**, SOMETIMES CALLED "BOXCAR" SENTENCES. THAT MEANS ONE SENTENCE DOES NOT BEGIN UNTIL THE ONE BEFORE IT ENDS. THE PRISON SYSTEM COMBINES CONSECUTIVE SENTENCES INTO A SINGLE SENTENCE WITH **ONE POST-RELEASE SUPERVISION PERIOD** AT THE END.

THEY WILL ADD UP ALL THE CONFINEMENT PORTIONS AND THEN ELIMINATE ALL OF THE PRS PORTIONS EXCEPT FOR THE LONGEST ONE. FOR EXAMPLE, IF AN INMATE HAD A 20-36 MONTH SENTENCE FOR A CLASS E FELONY FOLLOWED BY TWO 6-17 MONTH CLASS H FELONY SENTENCES, IT WOULD LOOK LIKE THIS:

ADD UP THE CONFINEMENT PORTIONS

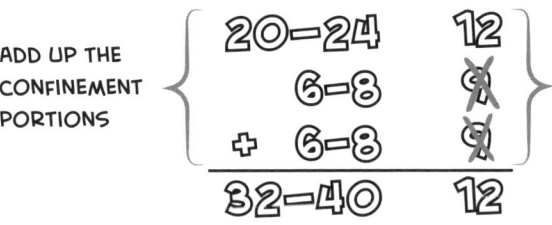

ELIMINATE ALL BUT THE LONGEST PRS PORTION

THE INMATE WILL SERVE BETWEEN 32 AND 40 MONTHS, DEPENDING ON EARNED TIME AND MERITORIOUS TIME, AND THEN BE RELEASED ONTO PRS FOR 12 MONTHS.

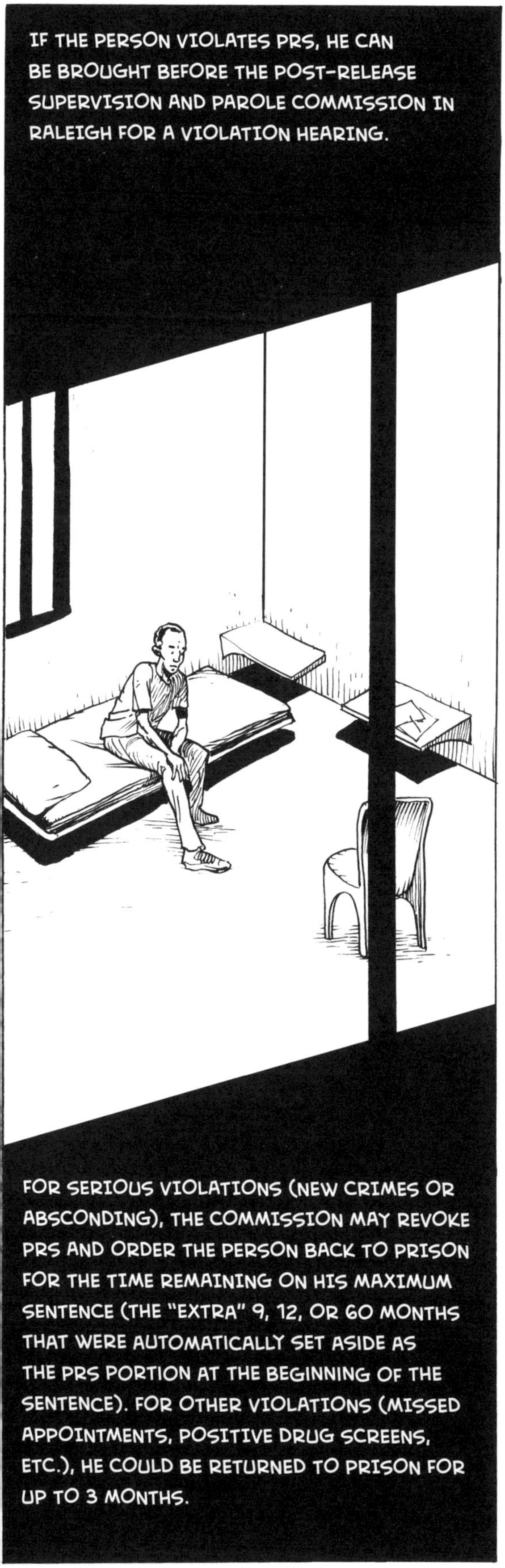

IF THE PERSON VIOLATES PRS, HE CAN BE BROUGHT BEFORE THE POST-RELEASE SUPERVISION AND PAROLE COMMISSION IN RALEIGH FOR A VIOLATION HEARING.

FOR SERIOUS VIOLATIONS (NEW CRIMES OR ABSCONDING), THE COMMISSION MAY REVOKE PRS AND ORDER THE PERSON BACK TO PRISON FOR THE TIME REMAINING ON HIS MAXIMUM SENTENCE (THE "EXTRA" 9, 12, OR 60 MONTHS THAT WERE AUTOMATICALLY SET ASIDE AS THE PRS PORTION AT THE BEGINNING OF THE SENTENCE). FOR OTHER VIOLATIONS (MISSED APPOINTMENTS, POSITIVE DRUG SCREENS, ETC.), HE COULD BE RETURNED TO PRISON FOR UP TO 3 MONTHS.

ONCE THE PRS PERIOD EXPIRES OR ALL THE TIME REMAINING ON THE REMAINING TERM OF IMPRISONMENT HAS BEEN SERVED, THE SENTENCE IS COMPLETE.

Jamie Markham is an associate professor of public law and government at the School of Government. He joined the faculty in 2007. His area of interest is criminal law and procedure, with a focus on the law of sentencing and corrections.

Shane Tharrington is the manager of classification and technical support for the prisons division of North Carolina's Department of Public Safety. He has worked in many capacities in the prison system for twenty-five years.

Jason Whitley is a painter, illustrator, and cartoonist. His portrait of Charlotte Hawkins Brown is in the Charlotte Hawkins Brown Museum. His newspaper comic strip, Sea Urchins, is collected into four books.

UNC
SCHOOL OF
GOVERNMENT

IN PRISON

9 781560 118992

90000

This publication was printed and assembled by inmates and staff at the Correction Enterprises Print Plant.

CORRECTION ENTERPRISES

Not Just Making It Right. Making It Better.

ISBN-13: 978-1-56011-899-2

2017.04

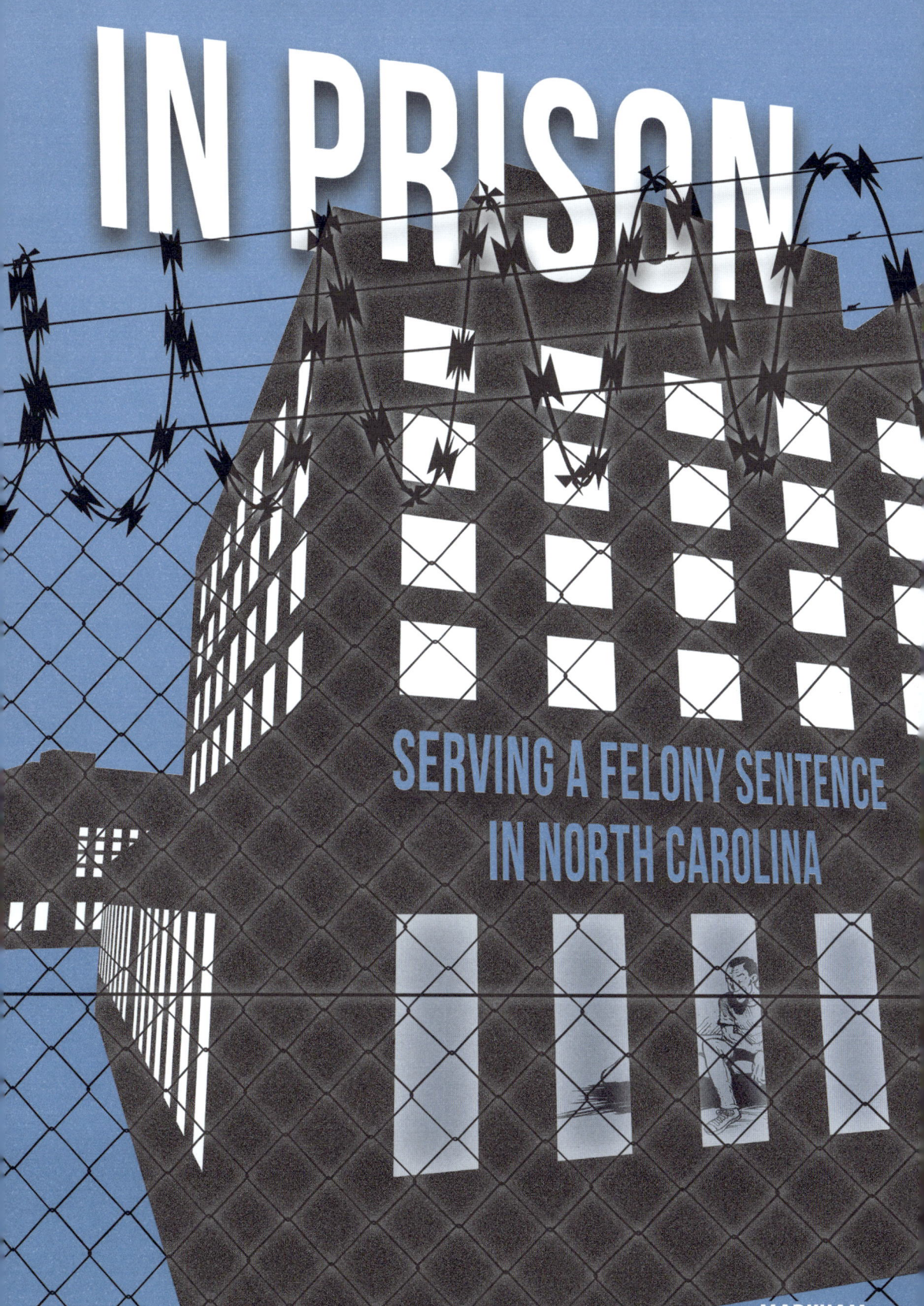

IN PRISON

SERVING A FELONY SENTENCE IN NORTH CAROLINA

MARKHAM
THARRINGTON
WHITLEY

The School of Government at the University of North Carolina at Chapel Hill works to improve the lives of North Carolinians by engaging in practical scholarship that helps public officials and citizens understand and improve state and local government. Established in 1931 as the Institute of Government, the School provides educational, advisory, and research services for state and local governments. The School of Government is also home to a nationally ranked Master of Public Administration program, the North Carolina Judicial College, and specialized centers focused on community and economic development, information technology, and environmental finance.

As the largest university-based local government training, advisory, and research organization in the United States, the School of Government offers up to 200 courses, webinars, and specialized conferences for more than 12,000 public officials each year. In addition, faculty members annually publish approximately 50 books, manuals, reports, articles, bulletins, and other print and online content related to state and local government. The School also produces the *Daily Bulletin Online* each day the General Assembly is in session, reporting on activities for members of the legislature and others who need to follow the course of legislation.

Operating support for the School of Government's programs and activities comes from many sources, including state appropriations, local government membership dues, private contributions, publication sales, course fees, and service contracts.

Visit sog.unc.edu or call 919.966.5381 for more information on the School's courses, publications, programs, and services.

INTRODUCTION

This short book explains how a felony prison sentence is served in North Carolina. I hope those who read it will gain a better sense of where and how an inmate serves his or her time.

Presenting the information in illustrated form is by no means intended to make light of a very serious subject. It is, rather, offered as an accessible way to fill gaps in knowledge and to address common misperceptions about the way sentences are served. It is meant to give crime victims, defendants, inmates, and their families an understandable resource that translates the words and numbers on a sentencing judgment into a practical reality.

Though the book is of course not a comprehensive legal reference, I hope it will be useful to lawyers and judges, too. An improved understanding of how a sentence is administered should help you advise your clients, negotiate your pleas, and craft your judgments in a way that achieves a more refined measure of justice in each case.

I have neither the technical expertise nor the artistic talent to create something like this on my own. For the former, I relied on co-author Shane Tharrington, classification manager for North Carolina's Division of Adult Correction. For the latter, I turned to Jason Whitley, a talented illustrator who works as a creative lead for instructional innovation at the Eshelman School of Pharmacy at UNC-Chapel Hill. Many thanks to Shane (and to the prison system as a whole) for answering my many questions, and to Jason for turning my stick-figure storyboard into a real graphic novel.

Jamie Markham
Chapel Hill
September 2017

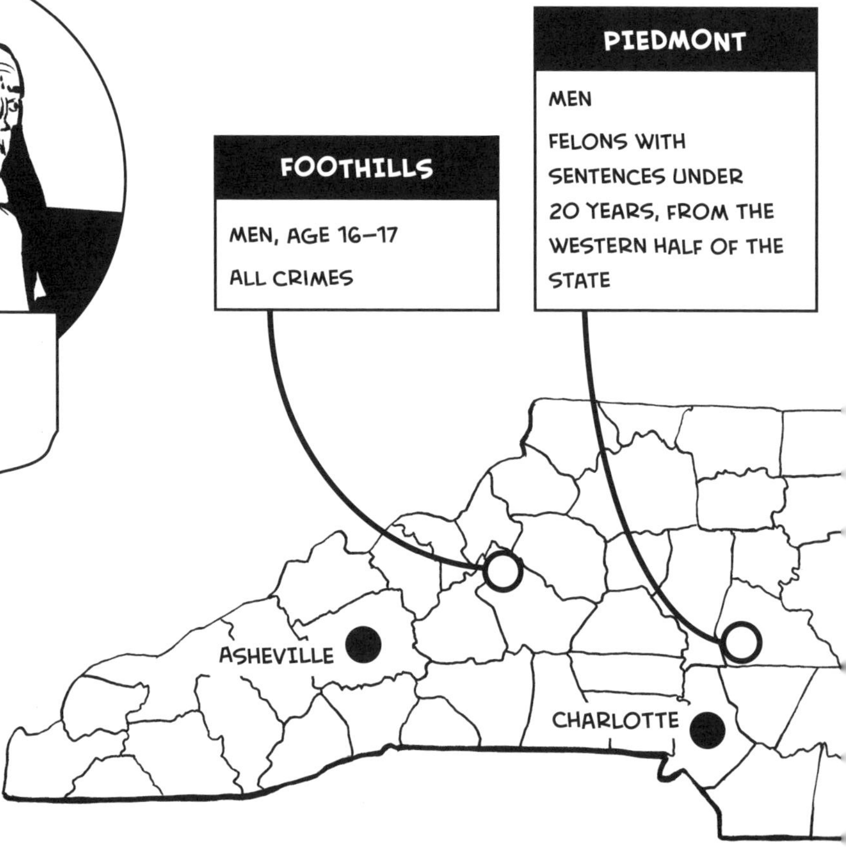

THE DEFENDANT WILL BE HELD IN THE COUNTY JAIL UNTIL THE PRISON SYSTEM PICKS HIM UP, USUALLY WITHIN A WEEK OR SO.

IF THE DEFENDANT APPEALS HIS SENTENCE, HE COULD BE RELEASED ON AN APPEAL BOND, BUT THAT IS RARE.

THE DEFENDANT'S FIRST STOP WILL BE ONE OF NORTH CAROLINA'S DIAGNOSTIC CENTERS.

PIEDMONT

MEN

FELONS WITH SENTENCES UNDER 20 YEARS, FROM THE WESTERN HALF OF THE STATE

FOOTHILLS

MEN, AGE 16–17

ALL CRIMES

ASHEVILLE

CHARLOTTE

NORTH CAROLINA'S DIAGNOSTIC CENTERS

THE DEFENDANT GENERALLY WILL GET JAIL CREDIT FOR ALL THE DAYS HE SPENT IN JAIL BEFORE CONVICTION.

JAIL CREDIT IS SUBTRACTED FROM BOTH THE MINIMUM AND MAXIMUM SENTENCE. FOR EXAMPLE, IF THE DEFENDANT HAD 2 MONTHS OF JAIL CREDIT, HE WOULD HAVE 8-19 MONTHS LEFT TO SERVE OF HIS 10-21 MONTH SENTENCE.

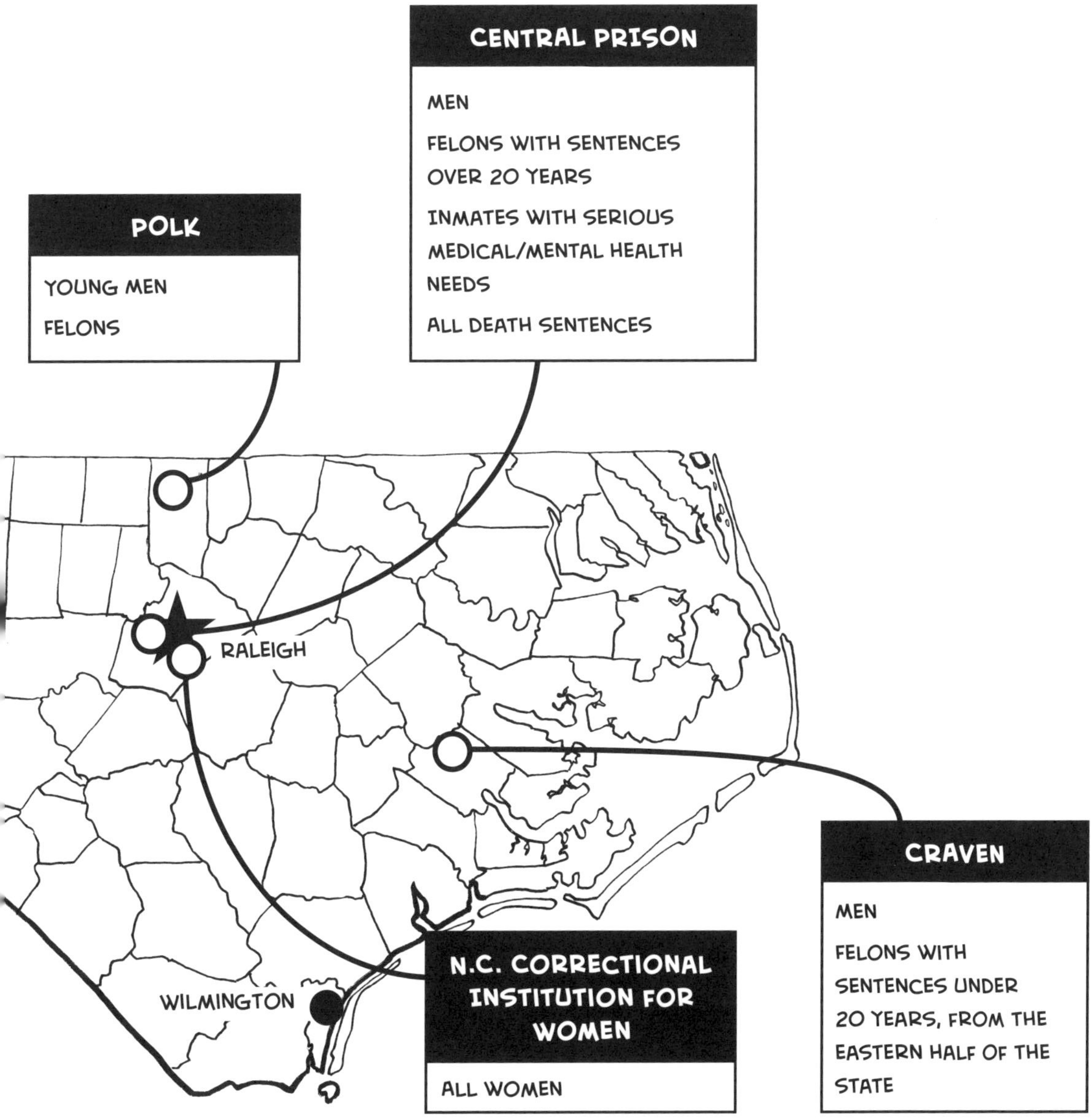

CENTRAL PRISON

MEN

FELONS WITH SENTENCES OVER 20 YEARS

INMATES WITH SERIOUS MEDICAL/MENTAL HEALTH NEEDS

ALL DEATH SENTENCES

POLK

YOUNG MEN

FELONS

RALEIGH

WILMINGTON

N.C. CORRECTIONAL INSTITUTION FOR WOMEN

ALL WOMEN

CRAVEN

MEN

FELONS WITH SENTENCES UNDER 20 YEARS, FROM THE EASTERN HALF OF THE STATE

THE DEFENDANT WILL SPEND 2–4 WEEKS AT THE DIAGNOSTIC FACILITY COMPLETING VARIOUS INPROCESSING ACTIVITES.

CLOTHING EXCHANGE

FINGERPRINTING

RISK-NEEDS ASSESSMENT

DNA SAMPLE

EYE EXAM

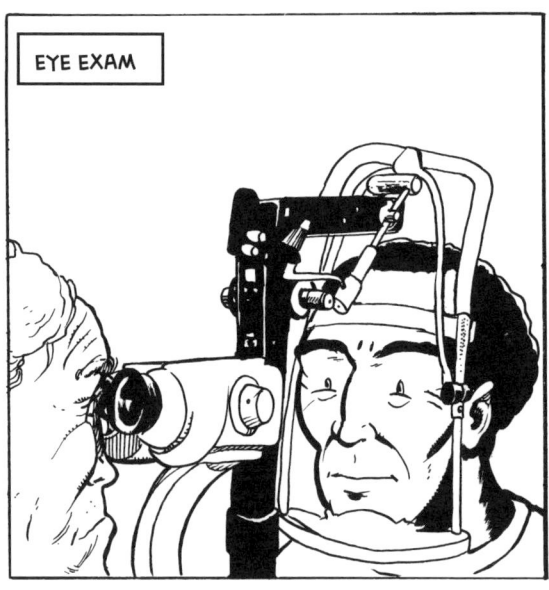

INTELLIGENCE TESTING

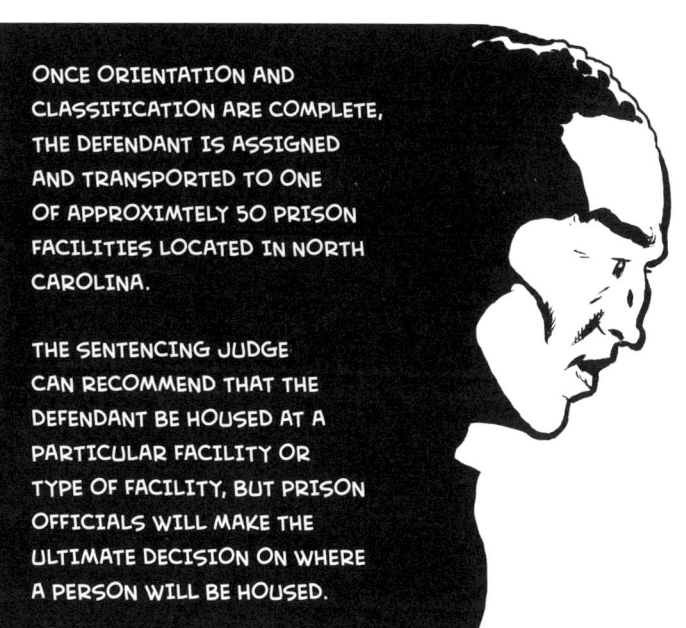

ONCE ORIENTATION AND CLASSIFICATION ARE COMPLETE, THE DEFENDANT IS ASSIGNED AND TRANSPORTED TO ONE OF APPROXIMTELY 50 PRISON FACILITIES LOCATED IN NORTH CAROLINA.

THE SENTENCING JUDGE CAN RECOMMEND THAT THE DEFENDANT BE HOUSED AT A PARTICULAR FACILITY OR TYPE OF FACILITY, BUT PRISON OFFICIALS WILL MAKE THE ULTIMATE DECISION ON WHERE A PERSON WILL BE HOUSED.

THE HOUSING DECISION IS BASED IN PART ON THE CUSTODY LEVEL TO WHICH THE INMATE IS ASSIGNED DURING CLASSIFICATION.

THERE ARE THREE MAIN CUSTODY LEVELS IN THE NORTH CAROLINA PRISON SYSTEM:

CLOSE CUSTODY (MOST SECURE)

MEDIUM CUSTODY

MINIMUM CUSTODY

THE MAP BELOW SHOWS SOME OF THE PRISONS TO WHICH AN INMATE MIGHT BE ASSIGNED. IT HIGHLIGHTS A SAMPLING OF THE SPECIAL PROGRAMS AND JOB ASSIGNMENTS AVAILABLE AT CERTAIN PRISONS. OVER THE COURSE OF SERVING A SENTENCE, SOME INMATES WILL TRANSFER BETWEEN FACILITIES AS CUSTODY LEVELS, WORK ASSIGNMENTS, AND PROGRAM NEEDS CHANGE.

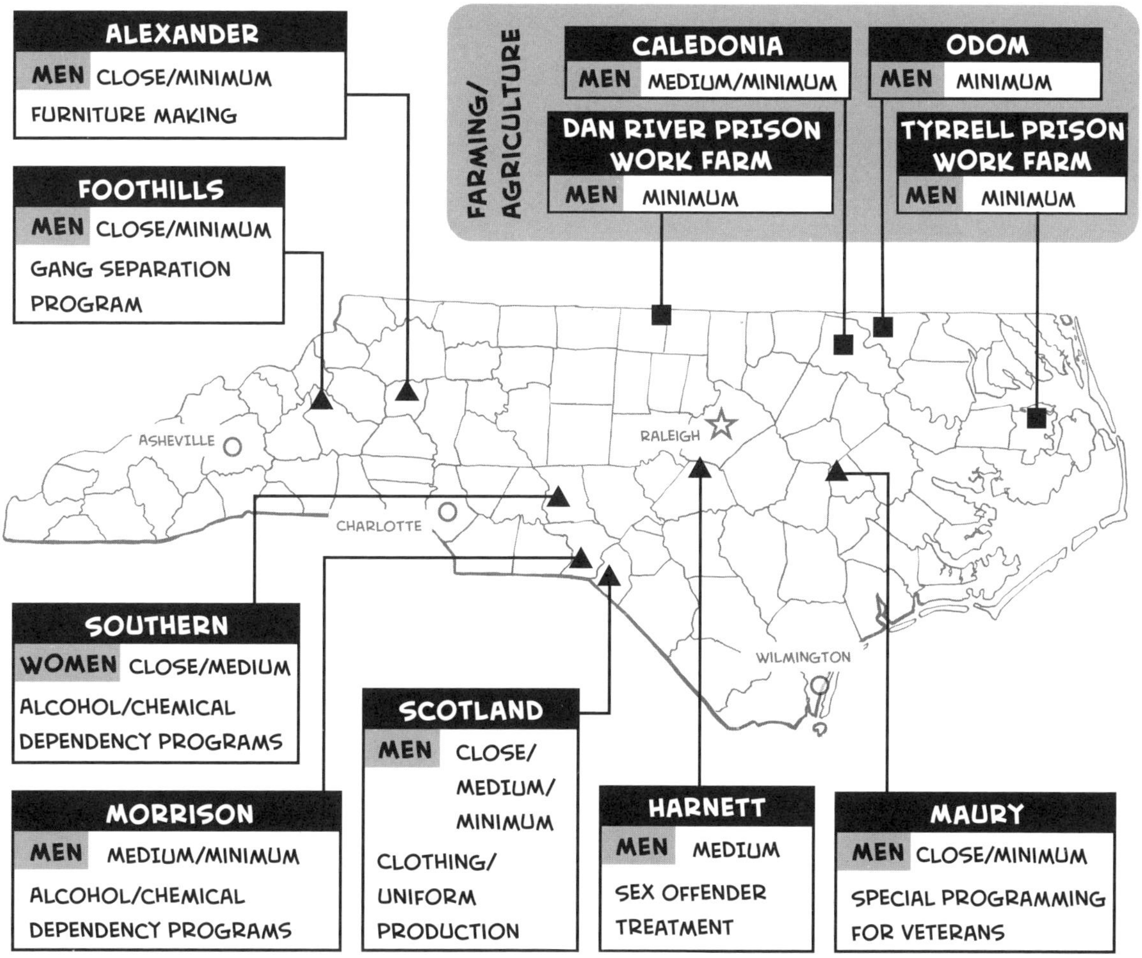

ALEXANDER
MEN CLOSE/MINIMUM
FURNITURE MAKING

FOOTHILLS
MEN CLOSE/MINIMUM
GANG SEPARATION PROGRAM

FARMING/AGRICULTURE

CALEDONIA
MEN MEDIUM/MINIMUM

DAN RIVER PRISON WORK FARM
MEN MINIMUM

ODOM
MEN MINIMUM

TYRRELL PRISON WORK FARM
MEN MINIMUM

ASHEVILLE

RALEIGH ☆

CHARLOTTE

WILMINGTON

SOUTHERN
WOMEN CLOSE/MEDIUM
ALCOHOL/CHEMICAL DEPENDENCY PROGRAMS

MORRISON
MEN MEDIUM/MINIMUM
ALCOHOL/CHEMICAL DEPENDENCY PROGRAMS

SCOTLAND
MEN CLOSE/ MEDIUM/ MINIMUM
CLOTHING/ UNIFORM PRODUCTION

HARNETT
MEN MEDIUM
SEX OFFENDER TREATMENT

MAURY
MEN CLOSE/MINIMUM
SPECIAL PROGRAMMING FOR VETERANS

AT THE ASSIGNED FACLITY, THE INMATE BEGINS SERVING THE REMAINDER OF HIS SENTENCE. HOW LONG IT WILL TAKE TO SERVE IT DEPENDS IN PART ON WHAT HE DOES IN PRISON. PARTICIPATION IN WORK AND PROGRAMS ALLOWS AN INMATE TO EARN SENTENCE CREDITS CALLED **EARNED TIME**.

EARNED TIME IS AWARDED AT DIFFERENT RATES DEPENDING ON THE TYPE OF WORK OR PROGRAM COMPLETED. IN GENERAL, PARTICIPATION IN ANY OF THE JOBS OR PROGRAMS SHOWN BELOW WOULD BE REWARDED WITH 9 DAYS OF EARNED TIME PER MONTH.

EDUCATIONAL PROGRAMS

LAUNDRY

LICENSE PLATES

CONSTRUCTION

CUSTODIAL WORK

AN INMATE AWAITING A WORK OR PROGRAM ASSIGNMENT GENERALLY GETS 3 DAYS OF EARNED TIME PER MONTH.

INMATES CAN ALSO GET ANOTHER CREDIT CALLED **MERITORIOUS TIME** FOR EXEMPLARY ACTS, LIKE WORKING IN BAD WEATHER OR COMPLETING AN EDUCATIONAL DEGREE.

WELDING

ROAD SIGNS

TREATMENT GROUP

DOG TRAINING

ROAD WORK

KITCHEN WORK

SO WHEN IS AN INMATE RELEASED?

FELONY ACTIVE SENTENCES HAVE TWO PARTS: A PERIOD OF CONFINEMENT IN PRISON, FOLLOWED BY A PERIOD OF **POST-RELEASE SUPERVISION** (PRS). PRS IS A PERIOD OF SUPERVISED RELEASE IN THE COMMUNITY, SIMILAR TO PROBATION.

THE LENGTH OF THE PRS PORTION OF THE SENTENCE DEPENDS ON THE INMATE'S CLASS OF OFFENSE AND WHETHER OR NOT THE CRIME REQUIRES REGISTRATION AS A SEX OFFENDER.

OFFENSE CLASS	PRS PORTION OF MAXIMUM
CLASS F–I	9 MONTHS
CLASS B1–E	12 MONTHS
CLASS B1–E SEX CRIME	60 MONTHS

THE PRISON SYSTEM AUTOMATICALLY SUBTRACTS THE PRS PORTION OF THE SENTENCE FROM THE MAXIMUM AND SETS IT OFF TO THE SIDE. THAT'S BECAUSE THE INMATE WILL SERVE THAT TIME ONLY IF HIS POST-RELEASE SUPERVISION IS REVOKED. THE TIME THAT REMAINS AFTER SUBTRACTING THE PRS PORTION IS THE CONFINEMENT PORTION OF THE SENTENCE—THE TIME THE PERSON WILL ACTUALLY SPEND IN PRISON.

↓ MAXIMUM SENTENCE ↓

SOME PEOPLE THINK ALL INMATES ARE RELEASED ONCE THEY HAVE SERVED THEIR MINIMUM SENTENCE. **THEY AREN'T**. INSTEAD, THE INMATE STARTS FROM THE MAXIMUM AND WORKS HIS WAY DOWN THROUGH EARNED TIME AND MERITORIOUS TIME.

EXIT

MINIMUM SENTENCE

THE MINIMUM SENTENCE IS JUST THE LOWER LIMIT ON HOW MUCH THE SENTENCE MAY BE REDUCED. IN OTHER WORDS, NO MATTER HOW MUCH WORK HE DOES OR HOW MANY PROGRAMS HE COMPLETES, THE INMATE WILL NOT BE RELEASED BEFORE SERVING HIS MINIMUM SENTENCE.

MOST INMATES ARE NOT ABLE TO WORK THEIR SENTENCES ALL THE WAY DOWN TO THE MINIMUM. AVERAGE RELEASE DATES FOR EACH CLASS OF FELONY ARE SHOWN IN THE TABLE BELOW.

OFFENSE CLASS	PERCENT OF MINIMUM SERVED UPON RELEASE...
CLASS B1–C	102%
CLASS D	103%
CLASS E	104%
CLASS F	105%
CLASS G	107%
CLASS H	114%
CLASS I	113%

NOTICE THAT INMATES WITH MORE SERIOUS CONVICTIONS GENERALLY DO A BETTER JOB OF WORKING THEIR RELEASE DATES DOWN TOWARD THE MINIMUM SENTENCE. WHY? IT'S BECAUSE MANY INMATES WITH SHORTER SENTENCES AREN'T IN PRISON LONG ENOUGH TO COMPLETE PROGRAMS OR GET PLACED IN THE JOBS THAT EARN A LOT OF EARNED TIME.

LET'S PUT IT ALL TOGETHER FOR OUR EXAMPLE OF AN INMATE SERVING A 10–21 MONTH SENTENCE FOR A CLASS G FELONY. THE LAST 9 MONTHS OF HIS SENTENCE WILL BE SET ASIDE FOR PRS, LEAVING 10–12 MONTHS OF CONFINEMENT TO SERVE. ON AVERAGE, AN INMATE WITH A SENTENCE LIKE THAT WILL SERVE 107% OF HIS MINIMUM (10.7 MONTHS IN THIS CASE) BEFORE BEING RELEASED ONTO PRS. THE EARLIEST POSSIBLE RELEASE IS 10 MONTHS. THE LATEST IS 12 MONTHS.

10–12 MONTHS

9 MONTHS

CONFINEMENT PORTION

PRS PORTION

A FELONY INMATE'S SENTENCE IS NOT COMPLETE UPON RELEASE. ALL FELONS SERVE A TERM OF POST-RELEASE SUPERVISION (PRS) AFTER THEY ARE RELEASED FROM PRISON. IT'S MANDATORY—THE INMATE CANNOT REFUSE IT. THE LENGTH OF THE PRS TERM IS GOVERNED BY THE TYPE OF SENTENCE.

OFFENSE CLASS	LENGTH OF PRS
CLASS F–I	9 MONTHS
CLASS B1–E	12 MONTHS
SEX CRIME	60 MONTHS

DURING THE TERM OF PRS, THE PERSON IS SUPERVISED BY A PROBATION/PAROLE OFFICER—THE SAME OFFICERS WHO SUPERVISE PROBATIONERS IN NORTH CAROLINA.

WHAT ABOUT MULTIPLE SENTENCES?

MANY INMATES ARE SERVING TIME FOR MORE THAN ONE CONVICTION.

BY DEFAULT, SENTENCES RUN **CONCURRENTLY**. THAT MEANS THE INMATE SERVES THEM ALL AT ONCE AND GETS RELEASED WHEN THE LONGEST SENTENCE IS COMPLETE.

A JUDGE CAN ORDER **CONSECUTIVE SENTENCES**, SOMETIMES CALLED "BOXCAR" SENTENCES. THAT MEANS ONE SENTENCE DOES NOT BEGIN UNTIL THE ONE BEFORE IT ENDS. THE PRISON SYSTEM COMBINES CONSECUTIVE SENTENCES INTO A SINGLE SENTENCE WITH **ONE POST-RELEASE SUPERVISION PERIOD** AT THE END.

THEY WILL ADD UP ALL THE CONFINEMENT PORTIONS AND THEN ELIMINATE ALL OF THE PRS PORTIONS EXCEPT FOR THE LONGEST ONE. FOR EXAMPLE, IF AN INMATE HAD A 20–36 MONTH SENTENCE FOR A CLASS E FELONY FOLLOWED BY TWO 6–17 MONTH CLASS H FELONY SENTENCES, IT WOULD LOOK LIKE THIS:

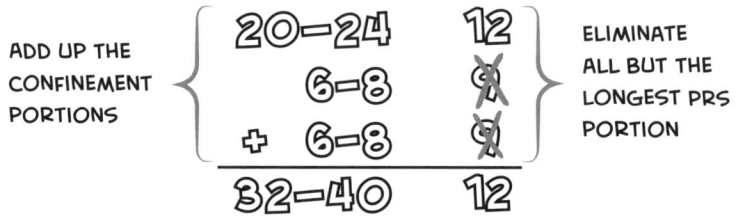

THE INMATE WILL SERVE BETWEEN 32 AND 40 MONTHS, DEPENDING ON EARNED TIME AND MERITORIOUS TIME, AND THEN BE RELEASED ONTO PRS FOR 12 MONTHS.

IF THE PERSON VIOLATES PRS, HE CAN BE BROUGHT BEFORE THE POST-RELEASE SUPERVISION AND PAROLE COMMISSION IN RALEIGH FOR A VIOLATION HEARING.

FOR SERIOUS VIOLATIONS (NEW CRIMES OR ABSCONDING), THE COMMISSION MAY REVOKE PRS AND ORDER THE PERSON BACK TO PRISON FOR THE TIME REMAINING ON HIS MAXIMUM SENTENCE (THE "EXTRA" 9, 12, OR 60 MONTHS THAT WERE AUTOMATICALLY SET ASIDE AS THE PRS PORTION AT THE BEGINNING OF THE SENTENCE). FOR OTHER VIOLATIONS (MISSED APPOINTMENTS, POSITIVE DRUG SCREENS, ETC.), HE COULD BE RETURNED TO PRISON FOR UP TO 3 MONTHS.

ONCE THE PRS PERIOD EXPIRES OR ALL THE TIME REMAINING ON THE REMAINING TERM OF IMPRISONMENT HAS BEEN SERVED, THE SENTENCE IS COMPLETE.

Jamie Markham is an associate professor of public law and government at the School of Government. He joined the faculty in 2007. His area of interest is criminal law and procedure, with a focus on the law of sentencing and corrections.

Shane Tharrington is the manager of classification and technical support for the prisons division of North Carolina's Department of Public Safety. He has worked in many capacities in the prison system for twenty-five years.

Jason Whitley is a painter, illustrator, and cartoonist. His portrait of Charlotte Hawkins Brown is in the Charlotte Hawkins Brown Museum. His newspaper comic strip, Sea Urchins, is collected into four books.

UNC
SCHOOL OF
GOVERNMENT

This publication was printed and assembled by inmates and staff at the Correction Enterprises Print Plant.

CORRECTION
ENTERPRISES

Not Just Making It Right. Making It Better.

IN PRISON

9 781560 118992

90000

ISBN-13: 978-1-56011-899-2

2017.04

IN PRISON

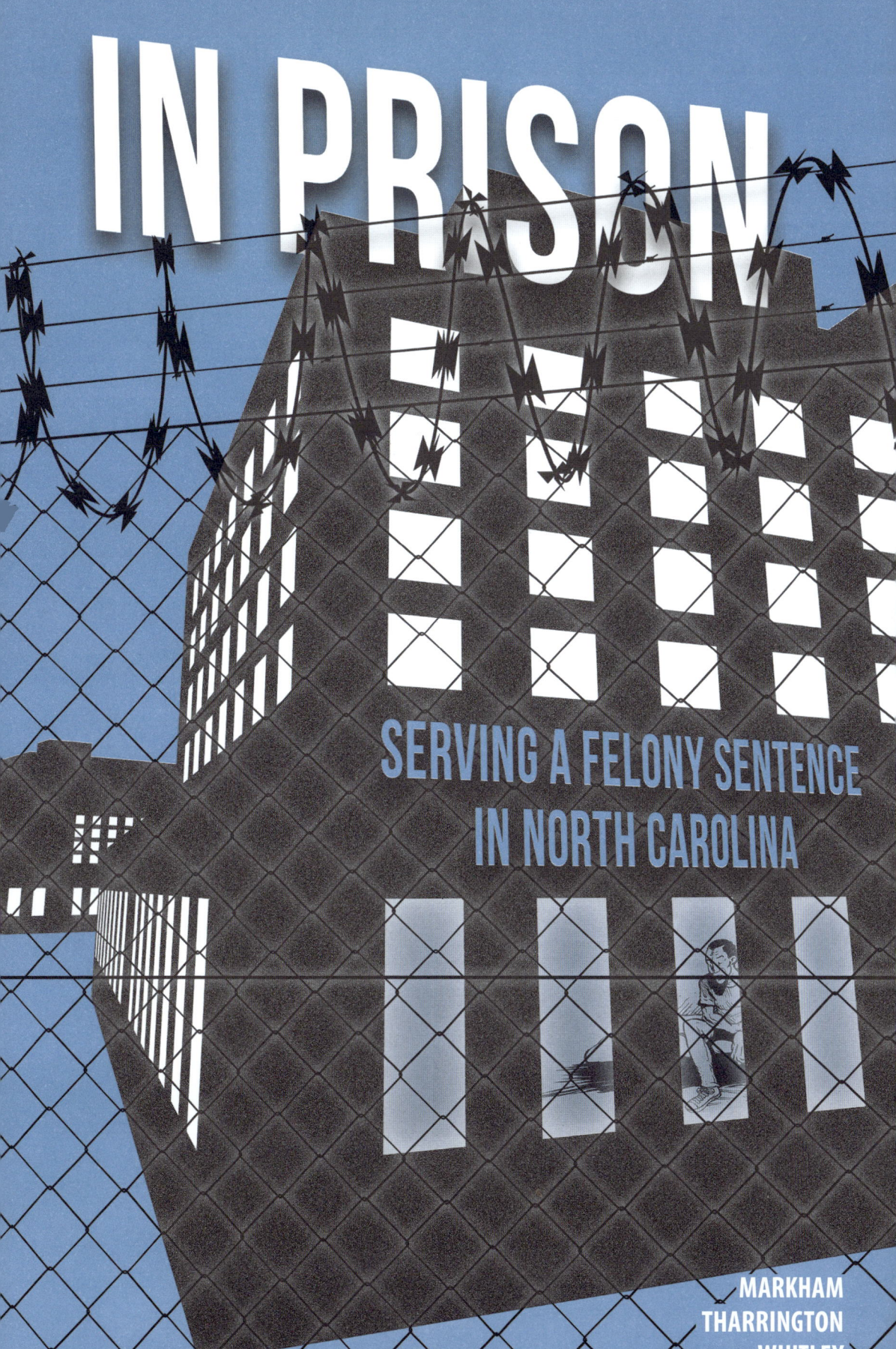

SERVING A FELONY SENTENCE
IN NORTH CAROLINA

MARKHAM
THARRINGTON
WHITLEY

The School of Government at the University of North Carolina at Chapel Hill works to improve the lives of North Carolinians by engaging in practical scholarship that helps public officials and citizens understand and improve state and local government. Established in 1931 as the Institute of Government, the School provides educational, advisory, and research services for state and local governments. The School of Government is also home to a nationally ranked Master of Public Administration program, the North Carolina Judicial College, and specialized centers focused on community and economic development, information technology, and environmental finance.

As the largest university-based local government training, advisory, and research organization in the United States, the School of Government offers up to 200 courses, webinars, and specialized conferences for more than 12,000 public officials each year. In addition, faculty members annually publish approximately 50 books, manuals, reports, articles, bulletins, and other print and online content related to state and local government. The School also produces the *Daily Bulletin Online* each day the General Assembly is in session, reporting on activities for members of the legislature and others who need to follow the course of legislation.

Operating support for the School of Government's programs and activities comes from many sources, including state appropriations, local government membership dues, private contributions, publication sales, course fees, and service contracts.

Visit sog.unc.edu or call 919.966.5381 for more information on the School's courses, publications, programs, and services.

© 2017
School of Government
The University of North Carolina at Chapel Hill

Printed in the United States of America

22 21 20 19 18   3 4 5 6 7

ISBN 978-1-56011-899-2

♾ This publication is printed on permanent, acid-free paper in compliance with the North Carolina General Statutes.

♲ Printed on recycled paper

INTRODUCTION

This short book explains how a felony prison sentence is served in North Carolina. I hope those who read it will gain a better sense of where and how an inmate serves his or her time.

Presenting the information in illustrated form is by no means intended to make light of a very serious subject. It is, rather, offered as an accessible way to fill gaps in knowledge and to address common misperceptions about the way sentences are served. It is meant to give crime victims, defendants, inmates, and their families an understandable resource that translates the words and numbers on a sentencing judgment into a practical reality.

Though the book is of course not a comprehensive legal reference, I hope it will be useful to lawyers and judges, too. An improved understanding of how a sentence is administered should help you advise your clients, negotiate your pleas, and craft your judgments in a way that achieves a more refined measure of justice in each case.

I have neither the technical expertise nor the artistic talent to create something like this on my own. For the former, I relied on co-author Shane Tharrington, classification manager for North Carolina's Division of Adult Correction. For the latter, I turned to Jason Whitley, a talented illustrator who works as a creative lead for instructional innovation at the Eshelman School of Pharmacy at UNC-Chapel Hill. Many thanks to Shane (and to the prison system as a whole) for answering my many questions, and to Jason for turning my stick-figure storyboard into a real graphic novel.

Jamie Markham
Chapel Hill
September 2017

THE DEFENDANT WILL BE HELD IN THE COUNTY JAIL UNTIL THE PRISON SYSTEM PICKS HIM UP, USUALLY WITHIN A WEEK OR SO.

IF THE DEFENDANT APPEALS HIS SENTENCE, HE COULD BE RELEASED ON AN APPEAL BOND, BUT THAT IS RARE.

THE DEFENDANT'S FIRST STOP WILL BE ONE OF NORTH CAROLINA'S DIAGNOSTIC CENTERS.

FOOTHILLS

MEN, AGE 16–17

ALL CRIMES

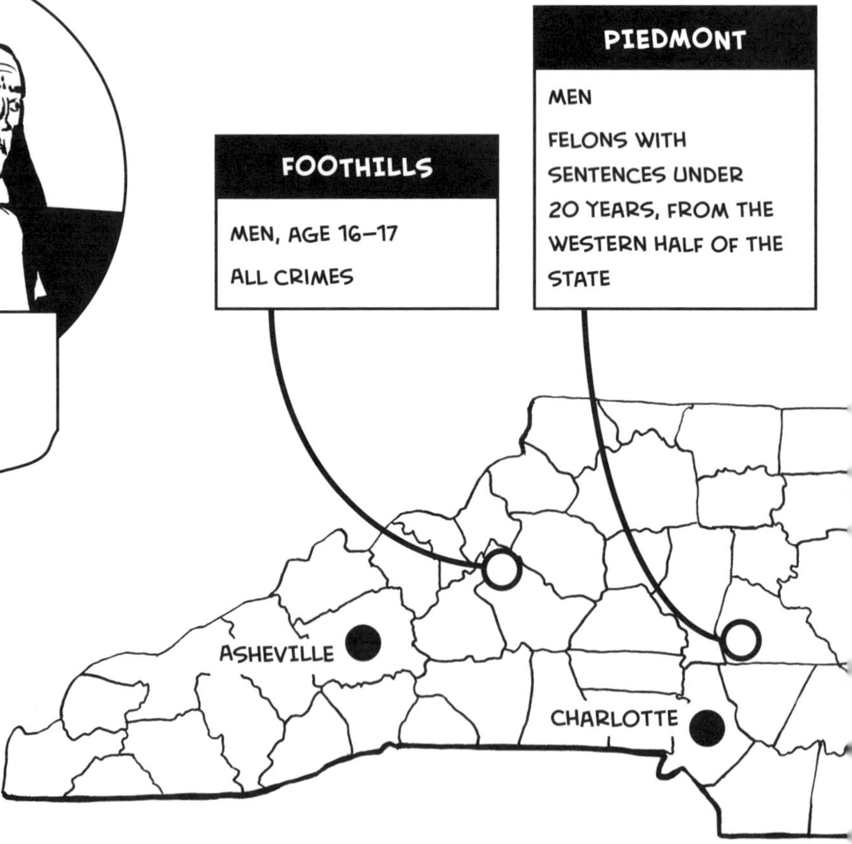

PIEDMONT

MEN

FELONS WITH SENTENCES UNDER 20 YEARS, FROM THE WESTERN HALF OF THE STATE

ASHEVILLE

CHARLOTTE

NORTH CAROLINA'S DIAGNOSTIC CENTERS

THE DEFENDANT GENERALLY WILL GET JAIL CREDIT FOR ALL THE DAYS HE SPENT IN JAIL BEFORE CONVICTION.

JAIL CREDIT IS SUBTRACTED FROM BOTH THE MINIMUM AND MAXIMUM SENTENCE. FOR EXAMPLE, IF THE DEFENDANT HAD 2 MONTHS OF JAIL CREDIT, HE WOULD HAVE 8-19 MONTHS LEFT TO SERVE OF HIS 10-21 MONTH SENTENCE.

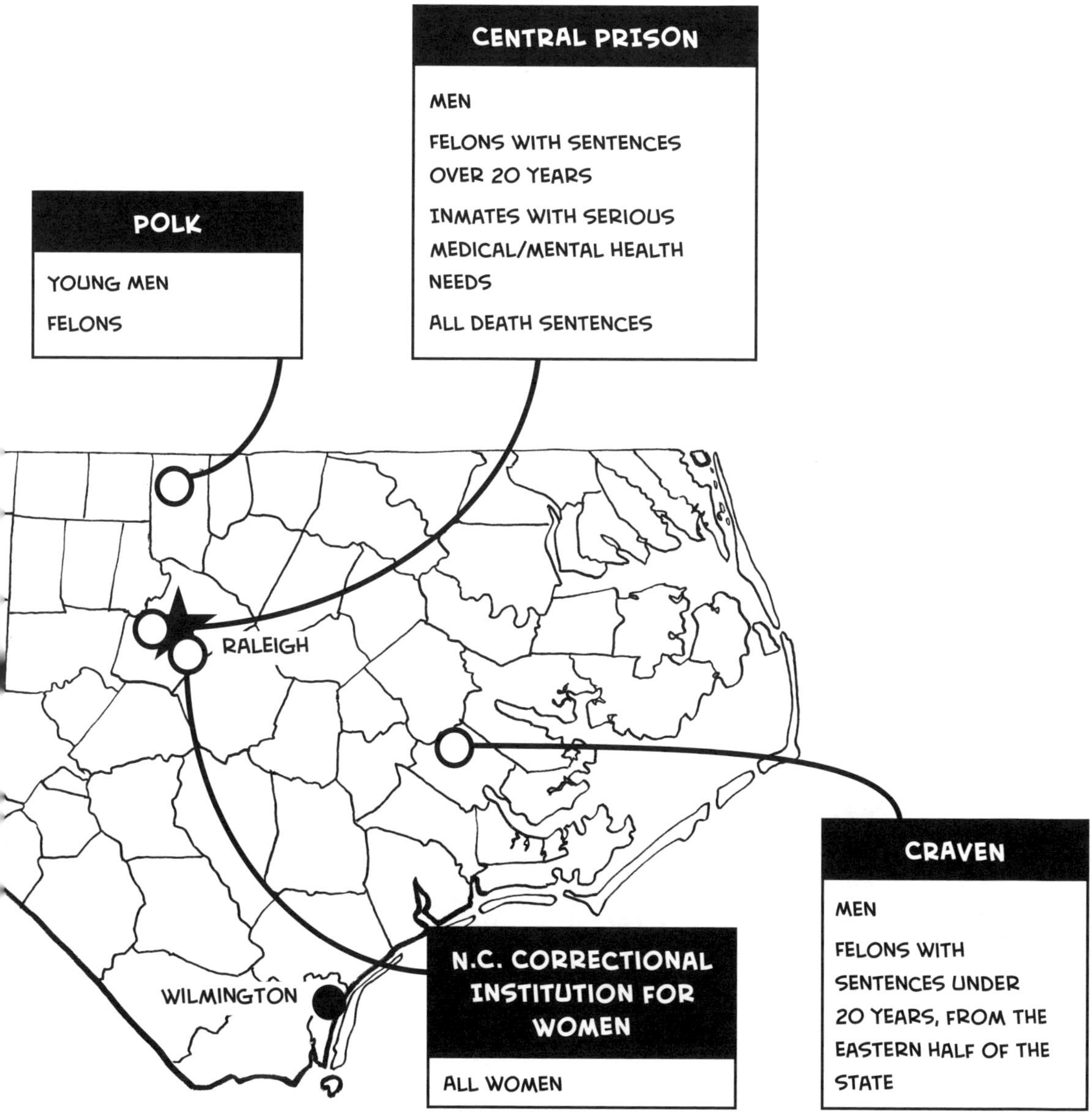

CENTRAL PRISON

MEN

FELONS WITH SENTENCES OVER 20 YEARS

INMATES WITH SERIOUS MEDICAL/MENTAL HEALTH NEEDS

ALL DEATH SENTENCES

POLK

YOUNG MEN

FELONS

RALEIGH

WILMINGTON

N.C. CORRECTIONAL INSTITUTION FOR WOMEN

ALL WOMEN

CRAVEN

MEN

FELONS WITH SENTENCES UNDER 20 YEARS, FROM THE EASTERN HALF OF THE STATE

THE DEFENDANT WILL SPEND 2-4 WEEKS AT THE DIAGNOSTIC FACILITY COMPLETING VARIOUS INPROCESSING ACTIVITES.

CLOTHING EXCHANGE

FINGERPRINTING

RISK-NEEDS ASSESSMENT

DNA SAMPLE

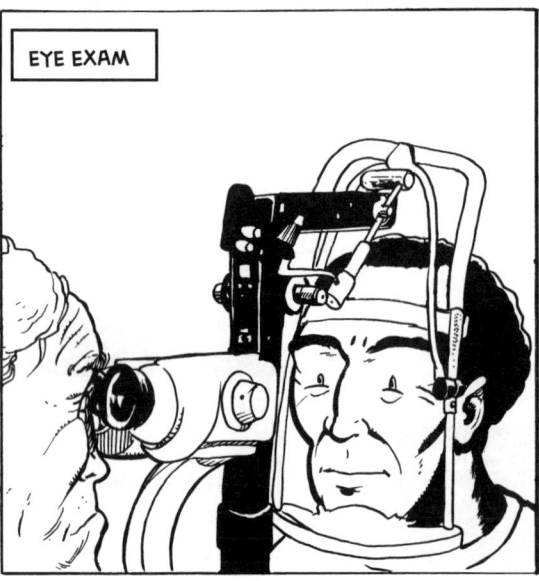

EYE EXAM

INTELLIGENCE TESTING

ONCE ORIENTATION AND CLASSIFICATION ARE COMPLETE, THE DEFENDANT IS ASSIGNED AND TRANSPORTED TO ONE OF APPROXIMTELY 50 PRISON FACILITIES LOCATED IN NORTH CAROLINA.

THE SENTENCING JUDGE CAN RECOMMEND THAT THE DEFENDANT BE HOUSED AT A PARTICULAR FACILITY OR TYPE OF FACILITY, BUT PRISON OFFICIALS WILL MAKE THE ULTIMATE DECISION ON WHERE A PERSON WILL BE HOUSED.

THE HOUSING DECISION IS BASED IN PART ON THE CUSTODY LEVEL TO WHICH THE INMATE IS ASSIGNED DURING CLASSIFICATION.

THERE ARE THREE MAIN CUSTODY LEVELS IN THE NORTH CAROLINA PRISON SYSTEM:

CLOSE CUSTODY (MOST SECURE)

MEDIUM CUSTODY

MINIMUM CUSTODY

THE MAP BELOW SHOWS SOME OF THE PRISONS TO WHICH AN INMATE MIGHT BE ASSIGNED. IT HIGHLIGHTS A SAMPLING OF THE SPECIAL PROGRAMS AND JOB ASSIGNMENTS AVAILABLE AT CERTAIN PRISONS. OVER THE COURSE OF SERVING A SENTENCE, SOME INMATES WILL TRANSFER BETWEEN FACILITIES AS CUSTODY LEVELS, WORK ASSIGNMENTS, AND PROGRAM NEEDS CHANGE.

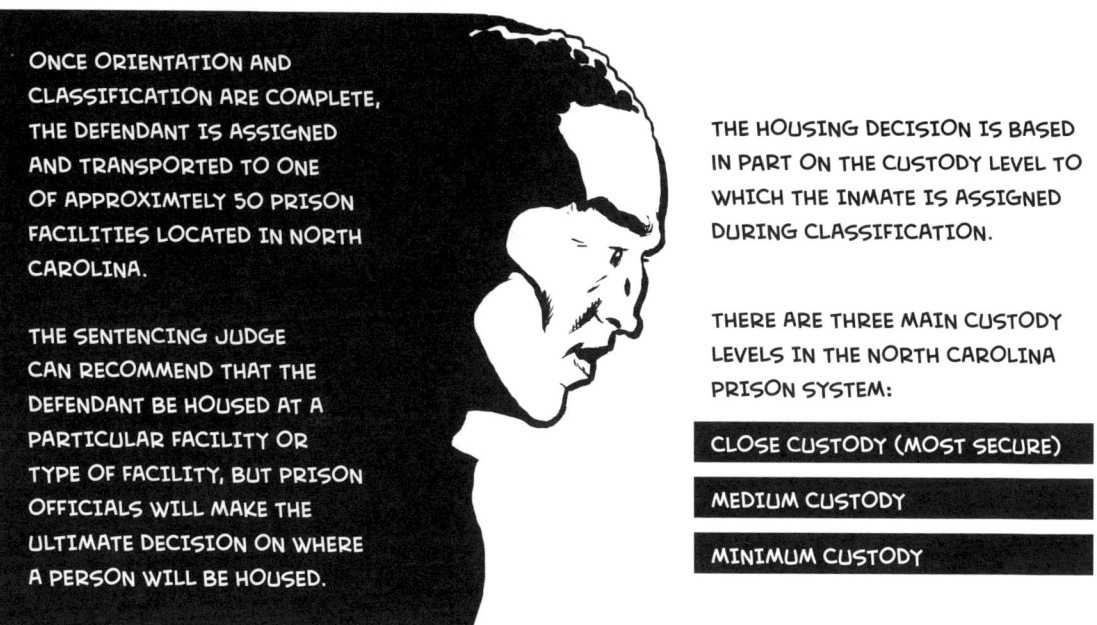

ALEXANDER
MEN CLOSE/MINIMUM
FURNITURE MAKING

FOOTHILLS
MEN CLOSE/MINIMUM
GANG SEPARATION PROGRAM

FARMING/ AGRICULTURE

CALEDONIA
MEN MEDIUM/MINIMUM

ODOM
MEN MINIMUM

DAN RIVER PRISON WORK FARM
MEN MINIMUM

TYRRELL PRISON WORK FARM
MEN MINIMUM

ASHEVILLE ○

RALEIGH ☆

CHARLOTTE ○

WILMINGTON

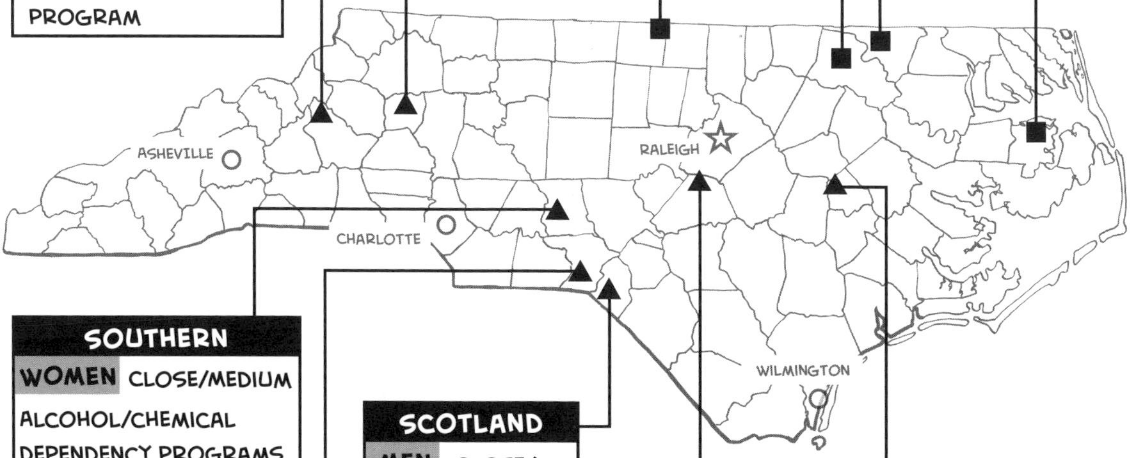

SOUTHERN
WOMEN CLOSE/MEDIUM
ALCOHOL/CHEMICAL DEPENDENCY PROGRAMS

MORRISON
MEN MEDIUM/MINIMUM
ALCOHOL/CHEMICAL DEPENDENCY PROGRAMS

SCOTLAND
MEN CLOSE/ MEDIUM/ MINIMUM
CLOTHING/ UNIFORM PRODUCTION

HARNETT
MEN MEDIUM
SEX OFFENDER TREATMENT

MAURY
MEN CLOSE/MINIMUM
SPECIAL PROGRAMMING FOR VETERANS

5

AT THE ASSIGNED FACILITY, THE INMATE BEGINS SERVING THE REMAINDER OF HIS SENTENCE. HOW LONG IT WILL TAKE TO SERVE IT DEPENDS IN PART ON WHAT HE DOES IN PRISON. PARTICIPATION IN WORK AND PROGRAMS ALLOWS AN INMATE TO EARN SENTENCE CREDITS CALLED **EARNED TIME**.

EARNED TIME IS AWARDED AT DIFFERENT RATES DEPENDING ON THE TYPE OF WORK OR PROGRAM COMPLETED. IN GENERAL, PARTICIPATION IN ANY OF THE JOBS OR PROGRAMS SHOWN BELOW WOULD BE REWARDED WITH 9 DAYS OF EARNED TIME PER MONTH.

EDUCATIONAL PROGRAMS

LAUNDRY

LICENSE PLATES

CONSTRUCTION

CUSTODIAL WORK

AN INMATE AWAITING A WORK OR PROGRAM ASSIGNMENT GENERALLY GETS 3 DAYS OF EARNED TIME PER MONTH.

INMATES CAN ALSO GET ANOTHER CREDIT CALLED **MERITORIOUS TIME** FOR EXEMPLARY ACTS, LIKE WORKING IN BAD WEATHER OR COMPLETING AN EDUCATIONAL DEGREE.

WELDING

ROAD SIGNS

TREATMENT GROUP

KITCHEN WORK

DOG TRAINING

ROAD WORK

SO WHEN IS AN INMATE RELEASED?

FELONY ACTIVE SENTENCES HAVE TWO PARTS: A PERIOD OF CONFINEMENT IN PRISON, FOLLOWED BY A PERIOD OF **POST-RELEASE SUPERVISION** (PRS). PRS IS A PERIOD OF SUPERVISED RELEASE IN THE COMMUNITY, SIMILAR TO PROBATION.

THE LENGTH OF THE PRS PORTION OF THE SENTENCE DEPENDS ON THE INMATE'S CLASS OF OFFENSE AND WHETHER OR NOT THE CRIME REQUIRES REGISTRATION AS A SEX OFFENDER.

OFFENSE CLASS	PRS PORTION OF MAXIMUM
CLASS F–I	9 MONTHS
CLASS B1–E	12 MONTHS
CLASS B1–E SEX CRIME	60 MONTHS

THE PRISON SYSTEM AUTOMATICALLY SUBTRACTS THE PRS PORTION OF THE SENTENCE FROM THE MAXIMUM AND SETS IT OFF TO THE SIDE. THAT'S BECAUSE THE INMATE WILL SERVE THAT TIME ONLY IF HIS POST-RELEASE SUPERVISION IS REVOKED. THE TIME THAT REMAINS AFTER SUBTRACTING THE PRS PORTION IS THE CONFINEMENT PORTION OF THE SENTENCE—THE TIME THE PERSON WILL ACTUALLY SPEND IN PRISON.

⬇ MAXIMUM SENTENCE ⬇

SOME PEOPLE THINK ALL INMATES ARE RELEASED ONCE THEY HAVE SERVED THEIR MINIMUM SENTENCE. **THEY AREN'T.** INSTEAD, THE INMATE STARTS FROM THE MAXIMUM AND WORKS HIS WAY DOWN THROUGH EARNED TIME AND MERITORIOUS TIME.

MINIMUM SENTENCE

THE MINIMUM SENTENCE IS JUST THE LOWER LIMIT ON HOW MUCH THE SENTENCE MAY BE REDUCED. IN OTHER WORDS, NO MATTER HOW MUCH WORK HE DOES OR HOW MANY PROGRAMS HE COMPLETES, THE INMATE WILL NOT BE RELEASED BEFORE SERVING HIS MINIMUM SENTENCE.

MOST INMATES ARE NOT ABLE TO WORK THEIR SENTENCES ALL THE WAY DOWN TO THE MINIMUM. AVERAGE RELEASE DATES FOR EACH CLASS OF FELONY ARE SHOWN IN THE TABLE BELOW.

OFFENSE CLASS	PERCENT OF MINIMUM SERVED UPON RELEASE...
CLASS B1–C	102%
CLASS D	103%
CLASS E	104%
CLASS F	105%
CLASS G	107%
CLASS H	114%
CLASS I	113%

NOTICE THAT INMATES WITH MORE SERIOUS CONVICTIONS GENERALLY DO A BETTER JOB OF WORKING THEIR RELEASE DATES DOWN TOWARD THE MINIMUM SENTENCE. WHY? IT'S BECAUSE MANY INMATES WITH SHORTER SENTENCES AREN'T IN PRISON LONG ENOUGH TO COMPLETE PROGRAMS OR GET PLACED IN THE JOBS THAT EARN A LOT OF EARNED TIME.

LET'S PUT IT ALL TOGETHER FOR OUR EXAMPLE OF AN INMATE SERVING A 10–21 MONTH SENTENCE FOR A CLASS G FELONY. THE LAST 9 MONTHS OF HIS SENTENCE WILL BE SET ASIDE FOR PRS, LEAVING 10–12 MONTHS OF CONFINEMENT TO SERVE. ON AVERAGE, AN INMATE WITH A SENTENCE LIKE THAT WILL SERVE 107% OF HIS MINIMUM (10.7 MONTHS IN THIS CASE) BEFORE BEING RELEASED ONTO PRS. THE EARLIEST POSSIBLE RELEASE IS 10 MONTHS. THE LATEST IS 12 MONTHS.

10–12 MONTHS

CONFINEMENT PORTION

9 MONTHS

PRS PORTION

A FELONY INMATE'S SENTENCE IS NOT COMPLETE UPON RELEASE. ALL FELONS SERVE A TERM OF POST-RELEASE SUPERVISION (PRS) AFTER THEY ARE RELEASED FROM PRISON. IT'S MANDATORY—THE INMATE CANNOT REFUSE IT. THE LENGTH OF THE PRS TERM IS GOVERNED BY THE TYPE OF SENTENCE.

OFFENSE CLASS	LENGTH OF PRS
CLASS F-I	9 MONTHS
CLASS B1-E	12 MONTHS
SEX CRIME	60 MONTHS

DURING THE TERM OF PRS, THE PERSON IS SUPERVISED BY A PROBATION/PAROLE OFFICER—THE SAME OFFICERS WHO SUPERVISE PROBATIONERS IN NORTH CAROLINA.

WHAT ABOUT MULTIPLE SENTENCES?

MANY INMATES ARE SERVING TIME FOR MORE THAN ONE CONVICTION.

BY DEFAULT, SENTENCES RUN **CONCURRENTLY**. THAT MEANS THE INMATE SERVES THEM ALL AT ONCE AND GETS RELEASED WHEN THE LONGEST SENTENCE IS COMPLETE.

A JUDGE CAN ORDER **CONSECUTIVE SENTENCES**, SOMETIMES CALLED "BOXCAR" SENTENCES. THAT MEANS ONE SENTENCE DOES NOT BEGIN UNTIL THE ONE BEFORE IT ENDS. THE PRISON SYSTEM COMBINES CONSECUTIVE SENTENCES INTO A SINGLE SENTENCE WITH **ONE POST-RELEASE SUPERVISION PERIOD** AT THE END.

THEY WILL ADD UP ALL THE CONFINEMENT PORTIONS AND THEN ELIMINATE ALL OF THE PRS PORTIONS EXCEPT FOR THE LONGEST ONE. FOR EXAMPLE, IF AN INMATE HAD A 20–36 MONTH SENTENCE FOR A CLASS E FELONY FOLLOWED BY TWO 6–17 MONTH CLASS H FELONY SENTENCES, IT WOULD LOOK LIKE THIS:

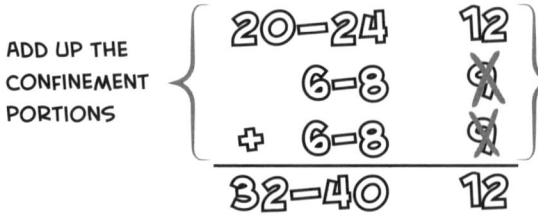

ADD UP THE CONFINEMENT PORTIONS

ELIMINATE ALL BUT THE LONGEST PRS PORTION

THE INMATE WILL SERVE BETWEEN 32 AND 40 MONTHS, DEPENDING ON EARNED TIME AND MERITORIOUS TIME, AND THEN BE RELEASED ONTO PRS FOR 12 MONTHS.

IF THE PERSON VIOLATES PRS, HE CAN BE BROUGHT BEFORE THE POST-RELEASE SUPERVISION AND PAROLE COMMISSION IN RALEIGH FOR A VIOLATION HEARING.

FOR SERIOUS VIOLATIONS (NEW CRIMES OR ABSCONDING), THE COMMISSION MAY REVOKE PRS AND ORDER THE PERSON BACK TO PRISON FOR THE TIME REMAINING ON HIS MAXIMUM SENTENCE (THE "EXTRA" 9, 12, OR 60 MONTHS THAT WERE AUTOMATICALLY SET ASIDE AS THE PRS PORTION AT THE BEGINNING OF THE SENTENCE). FOR OTHER VIOLATIONS (MISSED APPOINTMENTS, POSITIVE DRUG SCREENS, ETC.), HE COULD BE RETURNED TO PRISON FOR UP TO 3 MONTHS.

ONCE THE PRS PERIOD EXPIRES OR ALL THE TIME REMAINING ON THE REMAINING TERM OF IMPRISONMENT HAS BEEN SERVED, THE SENTENCE IS COMPLETE.

Jamie Markham is an associate professor of public law and government at the School of Government. He joined the faculty in 2007. His area of interest is criminal law and procedure, with a focus on the law of sentencing and corrections.

Shane Tharrington is the manager of classification and technical support for the prisons division of North Carolina's Department of Public Safety. He has worked in many capacities in the prison system for twenty-five years.

Jason Whitley is a painter, illustrator, and cartoonist. His portrait of Charlotte Hawkins Brown is in the Charlotte Hawkins Brown Museum. His newspaper comic strip, Sea Urchins, is collected into four books.

UNC
SCHOOL OF
GOVERNMENT

This publication was printed and assembled by inmates and staff at the Correction Enterprises Print Plant.

CORRECTION
ENTERPRISES

Not Just Making It Right. Making It Better.

ISBN-13: 978-1-56011-899-2
2017.04